Designing Accessible Websites and Applications

A Modern Approach to a More Accessible Web

Pavle Paunovic

Apress®

Designing Accessible Websites and Applications: A Modern Approach to a More Accessible Web

Pavle Paunovic
Kraljevo, Serbia

ISBN-13 (pbk): 979-8-8688-2003-8				ISBN-13 (electronic): 979-8-8688-2004-5
https://doi.org/10.1007/979-8-8688-2004-5

Copyright © 2025 by Pavle Paunovic

This work is subject to copyright. All rights are reserved by the Publisher, whether the whole or part of the material is concerned, specifically the rights of translation, reprinting, reuse of illustrations, recitation, broadcasting, reproduction on microfilms or in any other physical way, and transmission or information storage and retrieval, electronic adaptation, computer software, or by similar or dissimilar methodology now known or hereafter developed.

Trademarked names, logos, and images may appear in this book. Rather than use a trademark symbol with every occurrence of a trademarked name, logo, or image we use the names, logos, and images only in an editorial fashion and to the benefit of the trademark owner, with no intention of infringement of the trademark.

The use in this publication of trade names, trademarks, service marks, and similar terms, even if they are not identified as such, is not to be taken as an expression of opinion as to whether or not they are subject to proprietary rights.

While the advice and information in this book are believed to be true and accurate at the date of publication, neither the authors nor the editors nor the publisher can accept any legal responsibility for any errors or omissions that may be made. The publisher makes no warranty, express or implied, with respect to the material contained herein.

> Managing Director, Apress Media LLC: Welmoed Spahr
> Acquisitions Editor: Divya Modi
> Editorial Assistant: Gryffin Winkler
> Copy Editor: Kim Wimpsett

Cover designed by eStudioCalamar

Distributed to the book trade worldwide by Springer Science+Business Media New York, 1 New York Plaza, New York, NY 10004. Phone 1-800-SPRINGER, fax (201) 348-4505, e-mail orders-ny@springer-sbm.com, or visit www.springeronline.com. Apress Media, LLC is a Delaware LLC and the sole member (owner) is Springer Science + Business Media Finance Inc (SSBM Finance Inc). SSBM Finance Inc is a **Delaware** corporation.

For information on translations, please e-mail booktranslations@springernature.com; for reprint, paperback, or audio rights, please e-mail bookpermissions@springernature.com.

Apress titles may be purchased in bulk for academic, corporate, or promotional use. eBook versions and licenses are also available for most titles. For more information, reference our Print and eBook Bulk Sales web page at http://www.apress.com/bulk-sales.

Any source code or other supplementary material referenced by the author in this book is available to readers on GitHub. For more detailed information, please visit https://www.apress.com/gp/services/source-code.

If disposing of this product, please recycle the paper

To my wife, whose inspiration, patience, and encouragement guided me through this journey. To the wonderful people and my mentor I met in 2017, who inspired me to begin learning about accessibility.

Table of Contents

About the Author .... **ix**

About the Technical Reviewer .... **xi**

Acknowledgments .... **xiii**

Chapter 1: Semantic HTML **1**

   Introduction to Semantic HTML 1

      Pitfalls of Overusing <div> 2

      Div Soup 5

   Better SEO with Structured HTML 10

      Schema.org Vocabulary 12

      Maximize SEO with Accessibility Benefits 13

   Summary and Next Steps 15

Chapter 2: ARIA **17**

   Most Common ARIA Attributes 18

      Adding ARIA Roles Without a Behavior 20

      Conflicting and Redundant ARIA 21

      How a Nav Bar Works with ARIA 21

      Summary and Next Steps 33

Chapter 3: Colors and Accessibility **35**

   Why We Need to Pay Attention to Colors 36

   WCAG 36

      Use of Color (WCAG 2.1 SC 1.4.1) 36

      Contrast Ratio for Text (WCAG 2.1 SC 1.4.3) 37

      Common Pitfalls 37

      Colors and Forms 38

TABLE OF CONTENTS

    Colors and Charts 45

    Charts and Examples 47

    Contrast Analyzers 49

    Screen Reader Testing 49

    The Future 50

Summary and Next Steps 50

Chapter 4: Accessible Images 53

Importance of Alt Text 53

    Poorly Written Alt Text 54

    Well-Written Alt Text 54

More Tips for Writing Good Alt Text 55

Accessibility Standards for Images: WCAG and POUR 56

    Conformance Levels and Techniques for Meeting Image Requirements 57

    Types of Images and What to Look For 58

Alt Decision Tree 65

Summary and Next Steps 67

Chapter 5: Accessible Videos and Audio 69

Captions and Screen Readers 70

    Basic Accessible Media Controls 75

    Tools and Libraries for Captions 84

Accessible Audio Content 84

Summary and Next Steps 89

Chapter 6: Accessible Forms 91

Semantic HTML 92

Connecting with Labels 92

    Common Mistakes to Avoid When Labeling 94

Grouping Related Fields Together 94

    Common Mistakes to Avoid When Grouping 96

Keyboard Navigation 97

    Correct Usage of Tab Index in Forms 98

Testing the Keyboard Navigation 100
Tab Order and Screen Readers 100
Common Mistakes to Avoid 101
Accessible Forms and Error Handling 101
Summary and Next Steps 105

Chapter 7: SPAs and Modern Front-End Frameworks and Accessibility 107

React 108
Screen Readers and Basic Markup and Components 108
useState and Accessibility 114
useEffect and Accessibility 116
Testing and Linting 120
ESLINT Plugin JSX A11y 121
Vue 122
Screen Readers and Vue 123
The SPA Challenge 127
Testing and Linting 131
ESLINT Plugin: vuejs-accessibility 131
Angular 132
Frameworks and Choosing Your Path 138
Framework-Specific Strengths 139
Implementation Considerations 139
Summary and Conclusion 140

Index 141

About the Author

Pavle Paunovic holds a bachelor's degree in informatics/computer engineering and is a software engineer focusing on JavaScript and the Web with 10 years of professional experience. A software engineer by day, he is a guitar teacher by night. Through teaching people about programming and guitar, Pavle has developed a passion for sharing knowledge with people.

About the Technical Reviewer

Sivaraj Selvaraj focuses on modern technologies and industry best practices in his work. These topics include frontend development techniques using HTML5, CSS3, and JavaScript frameworks; implementing responsive web design and optimizing user experience across devices; building dynamic web applications with server-side languages such as PHP, WordPress, and Laravel; and database management and integration using SQL and MySQL databases. He loves to share his extensive knowledge and experience to empower readers to tackle complex challenges and create highly functional and visually appealing websites.

Acknowledgments

I would like to thank my wife for her endless support and inspiration throughout the writing of this book. My sincere thanks also go to the Apress team for their guidance, professionalism, and dedication, which made this book possible. I would also like to acknowledge the open-source community, who first inspired me in 2017 to learn about accessibility and whose contributions continue to shape and inspire my work.

CHAPTER 1

Semantic HTML

Introduction to Semantic HTML

HTML is the backbone of every website.

When we say semantic HTML, we mean HTML elements that are used for their intended purpose. In another words, you want to use right HTML elements for the right structure on the page.

Each tag in HTML needs to convey the role of content inside it. For example, <nav> is clearly used for navigation.

Using semantic HTML will make the structure of the web page more understandable developers and to the software/machines that people are using.

Writing accessible websites means creating online experiences that all people can use.

This includes users who have hearing impairments, visual impairments, and cognitive differences as well as people who rely on technologies such as screen readers, voice navigation, or specialized input devices.

One of the most significant ways to support these users right from the start is by writing semantic HTML.

People who are blind or have low vision use screen readers.

Screen readers read the structure of the web page.

By using HTML elements like <nav>, <main>, <header>, and <footer>, you help the screen reader jump to certain part of page, rather than going one element at a time down the page.

When developers use <div> for each part of the page, they must add extra classes, IDs, and complicated markup to achieve accessibility.

Semantic HTML reduces a lot this extra work.

CHAPTER 1   SEMANTIC HTML

Modern HTML provides elements to cover common parts of web application or page layout.

Here are some of them:

> **<header>:** For introductory or navigational information about the site or a specific section
>
> **<nav>:** For the site navigation and for major links
>
> **<main>:** For central content unique to a page
>
> **<section>:** For grouping related content withing a page
>
> **<article>:** For self-contained articles like news, blogs posts, etc.
>
> **<aside>:** For sidebars, pull quotes, etc.
>
> **<footer>:** For closing information, such as author of site, links, and copyright

Learn these well.

By learning these HTML elements and using them in your code, you turn the code into a **clear document outline** that users can navigate quickly.

Screen readers and other assistive tools automatically announce these regions with labels like "Navigation" or "Main Content."

This will help people with minimal effort find all the needed content.

While in this book we will focus on supporting people with disabilities, writing semantic HTML benefits everyone.

- Visual users will find it easier to scan for heading and sections.

- Search engines will better understand the thematic flow of your page, improving search engine optimization (SEO).

- Developers and designers working in your team can easily collaborate faster because the site structure is self-explanatory.

Pitfalls of Overusing <div>

When people are first learning HTML, after they discover the <div> element, they tend to use it for almost everything on page.

At first glance, it might by convenient to structure page using nothing but <div>s. It works visually, but it has several critical problems, especially when it comes to accessibility, readability, and long-term maintainability.

The <div> element does not have meaning or clarity. It tells the browser, the screen readers, and the developers nothing about what it contains. It's just a plain box. Without peeking inside <div> elements, we have no idea they represent headers, footers, articles, etc.

The <div> element is not evil per se. It is a little overused, but there are times when <div> element are perfectly valid to use such as when you need a generic wrapper or there is no suitable semantic element.

Badly Structured HTML Page

This is an example of a badly structured HTML page:

```
<div class="column-3">
    <div class="column-3">
        <div class="column-3">
            <div class="submit-button">
                <div class="button-text"></div>
                <div class="navigate">
                    <a href="#">Navigate</a>
                </div>
            </div>
        </div>
    </div>
</div>
```

This illustrates how *not* to write HTML.

The previous code has several issues:

- It uses nested <div> elements with class names instead of semantic elements.
- The submit button is a <div> instead of a <button> element.
- There is navigation inside <div> elements rather than a proper <nav> element.

- There is unnecessary <div> nesting.
- The structure is not really communicating what it is trying to convey.

Imagine how deep this can go. It is not good!

By contrast, the following is a good example of semantic HTML:

```
<section>
   <nav>
      <button>
         <span>Button Text</span>
         <a href="#">Navigate</a>
      </button>
   </nav>
</section>
```

This is much better.

Let me break down why. The section clearly indicates a thematic group of content:

`<section>` vs `<div class="column-3">`

It tells browsers and screen readers that this is distinct section of the page. The <div> element does not give us content meaning; it only suggests layout information.

The following explicitly defines a section containing navigation links, and screen readers can identify this as navigation:

`<nav>` vs `<div class="navigate">`

The <button> element is interactive by default. It can be focused on by keyboard and clicked and activated with a key. When screen readers see this button, they announce that its button.

`<button>` vs `<div class="submit-button">`

Let's look at another example of badly written HTML.

I call it *div soup*.

Div Soup

Here is the example of div soup:

```html
<div class="page-header">
      <div class="logo">Company Name</div>
      <div class="menu-container">
        <div class="menu-item"><div class="link">Home</div></div>
        <div class="menu-item"><div class="link">Products</div></div>
        <div class="menu-item"><div class="link">About</div></div>
        <div class="menu-item"><div class="link">Contact</div></div>
      </div>
    </div>

    <div class="main-content">
      <div class="article">
        <div class="title">Welcome to Our Website</div>
        <div class="date">March 4, 2025</div>
        <div class="content">
          <div class="paragraph">This is the first paragraph of our
          article.</div>
          <div class="paragraph">This is the second paragraph with some
          important information.</div>
        </div>
      </div>

      <div class="sidebar">
        <div class="sidebar-title">Recent Posts</div>
        <div class="post-list">
          <div class="post-item">First Post</div>
          <div class="post-item">Second Post</div>
        </div>
      </div>
    </div>

    <div class="page-footer">
      <div class="copyright">© 2025 Company Name</div>
    </div>
```

And here is beautiful semantic version:

```
<header>
    <h1>Company Name</h1>
    <nav>
      <ul>
        <li><a href="/">Home</a></li>
        <li><a href="/products">Products</a></li>
        <li><a href="/about">About</a></li>
        <li><a href="/contact">Contact</a></li>
      </ul>
    </nav>
  </header>

  <main>
    <article>
      <h2>Welcome to Our Website</h2>
      <time datetime="2025-03-04">March 4, 2025</time>
      <p>This is the first paragraph of our article.</p>
      <p>This is the second paragraph with some important
      information.</p>
    </article>

    <aside>
      <h3>Recent Posts</h3>
      <ul>
        <li><a href="/post1">First Post</a></li>
        <li><a href="/post2">Second Post</a></li>
      </ul>
    </aside>
  </main>

  <footer>
    <p>© 2025 Company Name</p>
  </footer>
```

Using div soup leads to an accessibility catastrophe.

Accessibility Catastrophe

Screen readers and other assistive technologies rely on semantic HTML to provide context and navigation options. Consider the following code for a news website built only with <div> elements:

```html
<!-- Inaccessible div version -->
<div class="news-page">
  <div class="site-header">
    <div class="site-title">Daily News</div>
    <div class="main-nav">
      <div class="nav-link">Home</div>
      <div class="nav-link">Politics</div>
      <div class="nav-link">Business</div>
    </div>
  </div>
  <div class="main-content">
    <div class="headline">Breaking: Important Event Occurs</div>
    <div class="byline">By Jane Reporter</div>
    <div class="article-text">The important event that occurred today...</div>
  </div>
</div>
```

For screen reader users, this creates several critical problems:

- **No document outline:** Screen readers cannot generate a hierarchical view of the headings for quick navigation.

- **Missing landmarks:** A user cannot jump from the main content to the footer, etc.

- **Bad or unclear interactivity:** Without proper link and button elements, it is not clear what is interactive.

CHAPTER 1   SEMANTIC HTML

In the following code, the <div> button is not focusable by default; it does not respond to Enter/spacebar keys and lacks proper role information:

```
<!-- Very bad -->
<div class="button" onclick="submitForm()">Submit</div>

<!-- Good: Keyboard accessible button -->
<button type="submit">Submit</button>
```

Fixing this requires JavaScript and accessible rich Internet applications (ARIA; more on ARIA in later chapters).

Why is the semantic version better?

- Proper document structure
- Navigation clarity
- Content hierarchy (<h1>, <h2>, <h3>)
- Semantic text (<p> instead of <div>)
- <article> used for main content, <aside> used for sidebar content
- Time element with machine-readable date/time attribute
- Uses proper <ul> and <li>

The semantic version is much easier to understand by developers and by screen readers, so it provides better accessibility.

Here are the steps for transitioning from div soup:

1. **Start with landmarks:** Replace main structural <div> elements with <header>, <main>, <footer>, etc.

2. **Add heading structure:** Properly tag headings with <h1> through <h6>.

3. **Fix interactive elements:** Replace <div> buttons and links with the proper elements.

4. **Test with assistive technology:** Verify the improvements with screen readers.

Here is an example transformation:

```html
<!-- Before -->
<div class="product-listing">
  <div class="product-card">
    <div class="product-title">Wireless Headphones</div>
    <div class="product-image"><img src="headphones.jpg" alt=""></div>
    <div class="product-price">$129.99</div>
    <div class="add-to-cart" onclick="addProduct(123)">Add to Cart</div>
  </div>
  <!-- More products... -->
</div>

<!-- After -->
<section class="product-listing">
  <article class="product-card">
    <h2>Wireless Headphones</h2>
    <img src="headphones.jpg" alt="Black over-ear wireless headphones">
    <p class="product-price">$129.99</p>
    <!-- Add click with in JavaScript script tag -->
    <button class="add-to-cart">Add to Cart</button>
  </article>
  <!-- More products... -->
</section>
```

When to Use <div> Elements

<div> elements are not all evil. They can serve important purposes for the following:

- Layout containers
- Grouping elements
- Implementation details hidden from users

  ```html
  <!-- Appropriate div usage -->
  <article class="product">
    <h2>Product Name</h2>
  ```

```
        <div class="product-gallery"> <!-- Justified div for layout -->
          <img src="product-1.jpg" alt="Product front view">
          <img src="product-2.jpg" alt="Product side view">
        </div>
        <p>Product description...</p>
      </article>
```

Better SEO with Structured HTML

Search engine optimization means improving your site's visibility to search engines so that your content can reach a wider audience.

One of most powerful tools for good SEO is well-structured HTML.

As you learned, structured HTML means writing markup in a way that clearly outlines the hierarchy and meaning of the content.

When search engines crawl your website, they analyze the HTML to understand the structure context of the content. A good and clear hierarchy helps search engines determine what the most important parts of the page are.

For example, a well-organized page with one <h1> tag followed by <h2> and <h3> tells search engines which parts of the main topics are supporting details.

Also, well-structured HTML makes it easier for search engines crawlers (also known as bots) to navigate the website.

Semantic elements create a natural path and landmarks that bots can follow, reducing the risk that they skip important content.

For example, using <nav> for your main menu helps crawlers quickly find links to other sections of the website, ensuring much better indexing.

A page that is accessible, easy to navigate, and logically organized enhances the user experience. Here are some tips:

- The <h1> tag is the most important heading of your page. It should describe the primary topic. In fact, using multiple <h1> headings is not good and can confuse search engines about the page's focus.

- Keep in mind div soup.

- Anchor links are the backbone of the Internet. They are fuel for the SEO.

- Focus on creating descriptive and consistent links between the pages. Building links between sites and pages is good for SEO.
- The text needs to be very descriptive.

Let me give you some examples.

Bad:

```
<strong>Cats and Guitars</strong>
<p>Cats, guitar</p>
```

Good:

```
<h1>Guitars</h1>
<p>There are electric and acoustic guitars. They are different</p>
<h2>Cats</h2>
<p>Cats are beautiful furry animals. Especially Tuxedo!</p>
```

In addition, you need to clearly describe images using the **alt** attribute so that they are meaningful to users relying on screen readers.

Properly describing images also helps search engines index image content accurately.

Bad:

```
<img src="cat.jpg" alt="" >
```

Good:

```
<img src="cats.jpg" alt="A beauiful tuxedo cat is playing with toy"  >
```

Further, please avoid (if possible) using generic links text like "click here." Describe link destinations clearly to enhance readability and context for users and search engines.

Bad:

```
<a href="products.html">Click here</a>
```

Good:

```
<a href="products.html">View All Products</a>
```

Also, make sure that your site/application is navigable using the keyboard alone. Clearly defined and structured navigation improves usability and mobility and is favorable for SEO due to ease of crawling.

Finally, make sure to keep layout intuitive and predictable, making navigation easier for both users and search engines crawlers.

Schema.org Vocabulary

Schema.org was launched in about 2011 as a collaborative project between Google, Microsoft, Yandex, and Yahoo to create a unified vocabulary for structured data.

This shared language allows website owners to provide explicit clues about the meaning of their content to search engines.

The Schema.org vocabulary consist of the following:

- **Types:** The categories of items we are describing (Person, Event, Product, etc.)

- **Properties:** Specific attributes that describe each type (name, address, price, etc.)

- **Values:** The actual data entered for each property

Schema.org and ARIA serve different but complementary purposes.

- **Schema.org** communicates content meaning to search engines.

- **ARIA** communicates content function to assistive technologies.

They can work together very nicely. Here's an example:

```
<article
  itemscope
  itemtype="https://schema.org/BlogPosting"
  aria-labelledby="post-title">

  <h1 id="post-title" itemprop="headline">Accessibility Best Practices</h1>

  <div itemprop="author" itemscope itemtype="https://schema.org/Person">
    <span itemprop="name">Alex Chen</span>
  </div>
```

```
  <div
    itemprop="articleBody"
    aria-describedby="content-description">
    <p id="content-description" class="visually-hidden">Article
    exploring web accessibility techniques</p>
    <!-- Content here -->
  </div>
</article>
```

You can learn more about this at Schema.org, where you can also validate your code: **https://schema.org/**.

Maximize SEO with Accessibility Benefits

Here are tips for maximizing SEO:

- Start with semantic HTML.

    Use elements that accurately describe the purpose of the content.

    ```
    <main>
      <article>
        <header>
          <h1>Article Title</h1>
        </header>
        <section>
          <!-- Content -->
        </section>
      </article>
    </main>
    ```

- Add ARIA attributes where native elements fall short.

    ```
    <div
      role="tablist"
      itemscope
      itemtype="https://schema.org/FAQPage">
      <!-- Tabs with FAQ content -->
    </div>
    ```

- Use Schema.org for search engines, not functionality.

  Note that Schema.org markup does not affect how elements function for users, only how search engines interpret them.

- Test with screen readers.

  Use screen readers and keyboard navigation to verify functionality.

  However, you need to make sure to avoid conflicts. While rare, potential conflicts between SEO and accessibility can arise.

  Some SEO tactics involve hiding content that's visible to search engines but not users, which can create accessibility issues.

  Solution: Make all content visible or use proper techniques like aria-describedby for additional descriptions.

- Focus on visual representation.

  SEO-optimized content sometimes prioritizes visual layout and logical structure.

  Solution: Ensure that the DOM order matches the logical reading order.

- To get both SEO and accessibility benefits:

  - Structured data testing tool: Validate the Schema.org implementation.
  - Wave or axe: Check for accessibility issues.
  - Screen reading text: Verify the content makes sense aurally.
  - Ensure all interactive elements like buttons are accessible.

Summary and Next Steps

You've completed Chapter 1. The following are the essential concepts that will serve as the foundation for everything you build:

- **Semantic HTML fundamentals:** You now understand how meaningful HTML elements convey structure and purpose.

- **Avoiding div soup and when to use <div> elements:** You recognize the accessibility problems that occur when you use only <div> for each element.

- **Improvements and basics of the SEO:** You know that a well-structured HTML page is a powerful tool for SEO.

- **From badly structured page to good**: You also learned how you can convert a badly structured page to good one.

- **Schema basics:** You learned about Schema.org.

Now that you understand what semantic HTML is, you're ready to learn about ARIA. In the next chapter, you will explore ARIA roles, states, and properties, as well as how they work together to create fully accessible web pages and applications.

CHAPTER 2

ARIA

Accessible Rich Internet Application (ARIA) is set of attributes designed to enhance web accessibility by supplementing HTML so that interactions with user who rely on assistive technologies like screen readers are accessible.

It bridges the gap where native HTML elements and semantics are inefficient, enabling developers to describe state, roles, and dynamic components clearly and accurately.

Proper use of ARIA improves the accessibility of web applications by making them usable for a broader audience. When I say broader, I mean people with visual, auditory, motor, or cognitive disabilities.

A screen reader cannot tell if a plain <div> is meant to be a slider or that an updating <span> is a live notification. ARIA can address this, as I said, to expand and supplement HTML so that assistive technologies will know what is happening on the page.

For example, HTML does not have elements for a modal dialog or a tree menu. With ARIA, you can set role="dialog" and role="tree" along with relevant properties to further define the purpose.

Keep in mind that excess ARIA attributes can confuse users.

The general principle is to always use native semantic elements first and then if necessary supplement them with ARIA. This is how to provide semantics to nonsemantic HTML.

Imagine if don't use ARIA and have functionality like show/hide, drag and drop, error messages, etc. Users who use assistive technologies would not know these elements were there.

ARIA is a defined set of roles, states, and properties that tie together important information needed for accessible web components. Roles define what an element is or does, states describe current condition of elements, and properties provide additional element characteristics.

ARIA roles define what an actual element is or what it does.

Many elements already have a role.

For example, a button has the role "button," and a heading has the role "heading." With ARIA you can set an element's role to:

- Give a nonsemantic element a semantic role
- Overwrite a role with a more specific one

For example, roles are categorized into types such as widget roles, landmark roles, document structure, and even more.

Landmark roles identify page regions to help with navigation. For example, use role="navigation" for a nav bar, role="main" for the main section of a page, and role="banner" for the main header area of the page.

Widget roles indicate that the UI controls and components are interactive, especially custom ones.

For example, role="slider" will be announced as a slider with a certain value.

You can use these roles when building custom control so the assistive technologies know how to treat them.

Document structure roles are less needed in the HTML5 era.

If you don't use HTML5, you can use role="article" and role="heading" as an example.

Note that giving an ARIA role does not impart any of the element's functionality automatically.

Most Common ARIA Attributes

A role attribute defines what an element does.

Let's look at the following example:

```
<div role="button" tabindex="0">Submit</div>
<div role="navigation">...</div>
<div role="search">...</div>
```

If possible, use <button>, <nav>, etc., and use ARIA when you cannot.

aria-label and aria-labelledby: When an element lacks visible text that explain its purpose, these attributes provide that crucial information.

```
<button aria-label="Close dialog">×</button>
<div id="heading">Account Settings</div>
<section aria-labelledby="heading">...</section>
```

aria-expanded: This indicates whether a collapsible element is currently expanded or collapse.

```
<button aria-expanded="false">Show more</button>
```

aria-checked and aria-selected: These communicate the selection state of checkboxes, radio buttons, tabs, and other selectable elements.

```
<div role="checkbox" aria-checked="true">Accept terms</div>
 <div role="tab" aria-selected="true">Profile</div>
```

aria-hidden: This hides elements from assistive technologies while keeping them visually present.

```
<div aria-hidden="true">...</div>
```

aria-live: This defines how and when change to and element should be announced by screen readers.

```
<div aria-live="polite">Status: Saving your changes...</div>
```

aria-required: This indicates that user input is required on an element before a form can be submitted.

```
<input aria-required="true">
```

aria-disabled: This communicates that an element is perceivable but not disabled, so it is not editable or otherwise operable.

```
<button aria-disabled="true">Submit</button>
```

aria-describedby: This identifies an elements that describes the object.

```
<input id="password" aria-describedby="pw-hint">
<p id="pw-hint">Password must be at least 8 characters</p>
```

Let's look at the following example of form validation:

```
// HTML
<label for="email">Email Address</label>
    <input id="email" type="email" aria-describedby="email-error">
```

CHAPTER 2   ARIA

```html
<div id="email-error" aria-live="assertive" class="error-message"></div>
```

```javascript
// JavaScript

function validateEmail() {
    const error = document.getElementById('email-error');
    // After validation logic...
    error.textContent = "Please enter a valid email address";
}
```

Remember to start with semantic HTML and use ARIA when you reach the point when it is necessary.

Remember when we talked about roles?

Here is an example of a widget role:

```html
<div role="slider"
    aria-valuemin="0"
    aria-valuemax="100"
    aria-valuenow="42"
    aria-valuetext="42 percent"
    tabindex="0">
  <div class="slider-handle"></div>
</div>
```

But be aware of ARIA pitfalls. As mentioned, it is better to use none than to use them incorrectly.

Adding ARIA Roles Without a Behavior

Here is an example of adding ARIA roles without a behavior:

```html
<!-- BAD: Role with no keyboard support -->
<div role="button">Click me</div>

<!-- GOOD: Role with keyboard support -->
<div role="button" tabindex="0">
  Click me
</div>
```

Conflicting and Redundant ARIA

Here is an example of ARIA roles that conflict:

```
<!-- BAD: Redundant and potentially conflicting -->
<button role="button" aria-pressed="true">Toggle</button>

<!-- GOOD: Native button with state -->
<button aria-pressed="true">Toggle</button>
```

You may be wondering how to know when ARIA actually helps. Well, you need to test it systematically.

1. Use VoiceOver (MAC), NDVA, or JAWS(Windows) or TalkBack (Android).
2. Navigate through the interface using just the keyboard.
3. Verify announcements to match your expectations.
4. Ensure all interactive elements can be reached via the Tab key.
5. Verify that the appropriate keyboard shortcuts work.
6. Check that the focus is visible indicated throughout.
7. Use the browser tools (F12).
8. Validate that the dynamic ARIA changes are reflected correctly.

How a Nav Bar Works with ARIA

The navigation nav bar is important in websites and applications.

Navigation is more than collection of links. It is road map for your entire interface.

For the users of assistive technology, properly implemented navigation can mean the difference between a usable app/site or very bad one.

Basic Navigation Structure

In the following example, the <nav> element communicates that this is a navigation region, but aria-label provides additional context when there multiple navigation sections on a page:

```
<nav aria-label="Main">
  <ul>
    <li><a href="/">Home</a></li>
    <li><a href="/products">Products</a></li>
    <li><a href="/about">About</a></li>
    <li><a href="/contact">Contact</a></li>
  </ul>
</nav>
```

Users need to know where they are in a site's hierarchy.

The aria-current="page" attribute announces to screen reader users which page is currently active, matching the visual indication (often different color, underline, etc.) that sighted users can see.

```
<nav aria-label="Main">
  <ul>
    <li><a href="/">Home</a></li>
    <li><a href="/products" aria-current="page">Products</a></li>
    <li><a href="/about">About</a></li>
    <li><a href="/contact">Contact</a></li>
  </ul>
</nav>
```

Drop-Down Navigation Menus

Navigation often includes drop-down menus, which require additional ARIA attributes to be fully accessible.

```
--------------- HTML----------------
<nav aria-label="Main">
  <ul>
    <li><a href="/">Home</a></li>

    <li>
      <button aria-expanded="false" aria-haspopup="true" aria-controls="products-menu">
        Products
```

```
          <span aria-hidden="true">▼</span>
        </button>

        <ul id="products-menu" role="menu" hidden>
          <li role="none">
            <a href="/products/software" role="menuitem">Software</a>
          </li>
          <li role="none">
            <a href="/products/hardware" role="menuitem">Hardware</a>
          </li>
          <li role="none">
            <a href="/products/services" role="menuitem">Services</a>
          </li>
        </ul>
      </li>

      <li><a href="/about">About</a></li>
      <li><a href="/contact">Contact</a></li>
    </ul>
  </nav>
```

-------------- JavaScript ------------

```
document.querySelectorAll('nav button[aria-haspopup]').forEach(button => {
  const menu = document.getElementById(button.getAttribute('aria-controls'));

  button.addEventListener('click', () => {
    const expanded = button.getAttribute('aria-expanded') === 'true';
    button.setAttribute('aria-expanded', !expanded);
    menu.hidden = expanded;

    if (!expanded) {
      const firstItem = menu.querySelector('[role="menuitem"]');
      if (firstItem) firstItem.focus();
    }
  });
```

CHAPTER 2   ARIA

```
  menu.addEventListener('keydown', (event) => {
  const items = Array.from(menu.querySelectorAll('[role="menuitem"]'));
    const currentIndex = items.indexOf(document.activeElement);

    switch (event.key) {
      case 'ArrowDown':
        event.preventDefault();
        items[(currentIndex + 1) % items.length].focus();
        break;
      case 'ArrowUp':
        event.preventDefault();
        items[(currentIndex - 1 + items.length) % items.length].focus();
        break;
      case 'Escape':
        button.setAttribute('aria-expanded', 'false');
        menu.hidden = true;
        button.focus();
        break;
    }
  });

  document.addEventListener('focusin', (event) => {
    if (menu.hidden === false && !menu.contains(event.target) && event.
    target !== button) {
      button.setAttribute('aria-expanded', 'false');
      menu.hidden = true;
    }
  });
})
```

This implementation includes several critical ARIA features:

> **aria-expanded:** Indicates whether the drop-down menu is open or closed

> **aria-haspopup:** Tells screen reader that activating this control will display a menu

aria-controls: Creates a programmatic relationship between the button and the menu controls

role="menu" and role="menuitem": Identifies the drop-down as a menu structure

role="none": Applied to list items to prevent the screen reader from announcing them as list items when they're serving as structural containers

Common Navigation Pitfalls with ARIA

The following are some common pitfalls:

- **Missing ARIA states during dynamic changes:** Always update ARIA states when the UI changes.

    ```
    // INCORRECT: UI changes without ARIA updates
    toggleButton.addEventListener('click', () => {
      menu.classList.toggle('visible');
    });

    // CORRECT: ARIA states updated with visual changes
    toggleButton.addEventListener('click', () => {
      const isExpanded = toggleButton.getAttribute('aria-expanded') === 'true';
      toggleButton.setAttribute('aria-expanded', !isExpanded);
      menu.classList.toggle('visible');
      menu.hidden = isExpanded;
    });
    ```

- **Keyboard traps:** Ensure users can both enter and exit navigation components.

    ```
    // INCORRECT: No way to exit the menu with keyboard
    menuItems.forEach(item => {
      item.addEventListener('keydown', (event) => {
        if (event.key === 'ArrowDown') {
          // Move to next item
    ```

```
          event.preventDefault();
          // No escape handling
        }
      });
    });

    // CORRECT: Allow exiting navigation
    menuItems.forEach(item => {
      item.addEventListener('keydown', (event) => {
        if (event.key === 'ArrowDown') {
          // Move to next item
          event.preventDefault();
        } else if (event.key === 'Escape') {
          // Exit the menu
          closeMenu();
          menuButton.focus();
        }
      });
    });
```

Navigation is not only about links. It's about creating a coherent map of applications.

By combining semantic HTML elements, appropriate HTML attributes, and careful keyboard navigation, you can create navigation systems that work for everyone, regardless of how they access or navigate the Web.

Combining ARIA with HTML and JavaScript

The ARIA is not meant to work in isolation. Think of it of three-part harmony.

- **HTML** provides a semantic structure.
- **ARIA** enhances semantics.
- **JavaScript** brings everything to life.

At its core, web accessibility relies on three interconnected technologies working together.

CHAPTER 2　ARIA

When you visit a website, a browser creates something called an *accessibility tree*. This tree is a simplified version of the DOM that is exposed to assistive technologies through the platform accessibility API.

For example, in Firefox, when you open Developers Tools, you can see the accessibility tree (Figure 2-1).

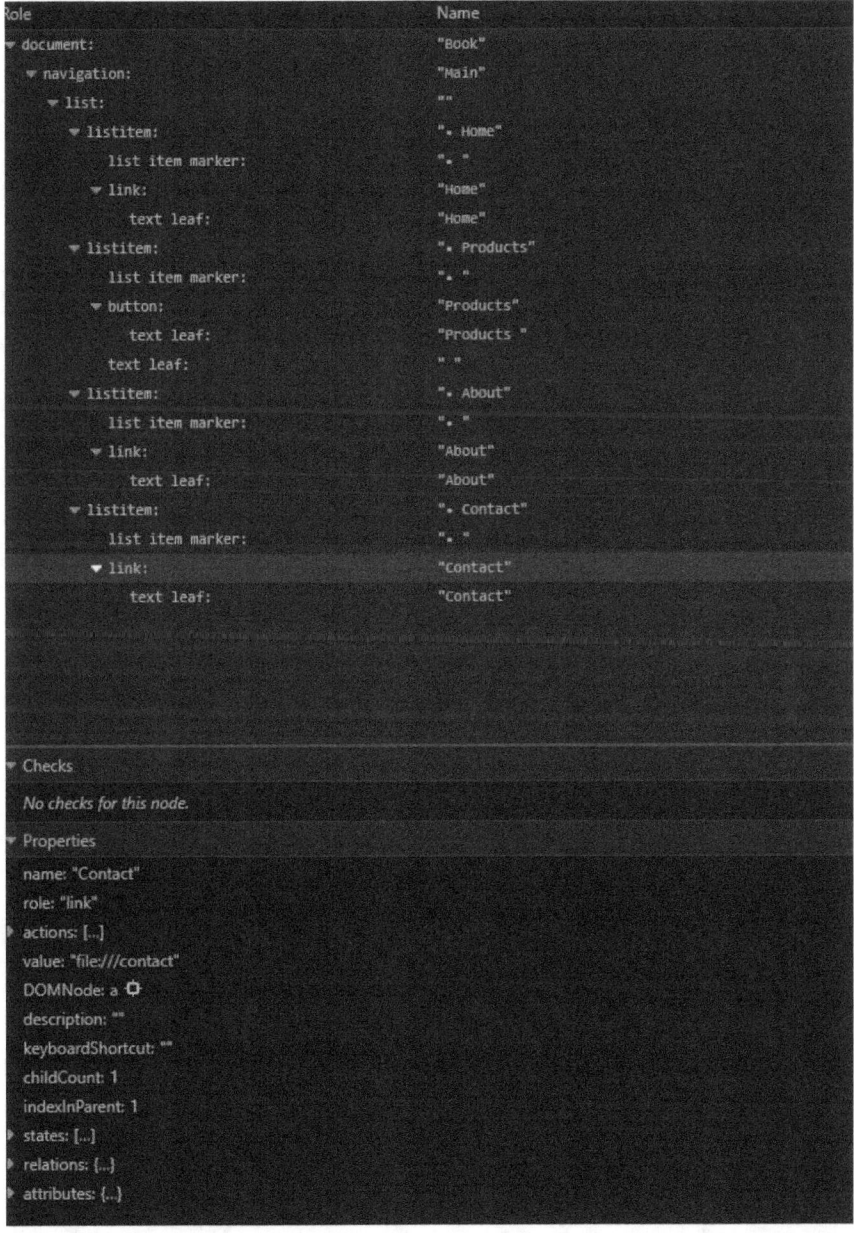

Figure 2-1. *Browser tools console*

This accessibility tree communicates the following:

- What type of element something is (role)
- Its properties (name, description)
- Its current state (checked, unchecked, etc.)
- Its relationship to other elements

Modal Implementation

Modals are always complex to implement with accessibility. Here is an example:

```html
<!-- Trigger button -->
<button id="open-dialog" aria-haspopup="dialog">Open Settings</button>

<!-- The modal dialog -->
<div id="settings-dialog"
    role="dialog"
    aria-labelledby="dialog-title"
    aria-describedby="dialog-desc"
    aria-modal="true"
    hidden>

  <div class="dialog-content">
    <header>
      <h2 id="dialog-title">Application Settings</h2>
      <button aria-label="Close dialog" class="close-button">×</button>
    </header>

    <div id="dialog-desc" class="sr-only">
      Configure your application preferences and settings
    </div>

    <main>
      <form>
        <fieldset>
          <legend>Display Options</legend>
```

```html
      <div class="form-group">
        <input type="checkbox" id="dark-mode" name="dark-mode">
        <label for="dark-mode">Dark Mode</label>
      </div>

      <div class="form-group">
        <label for="font-size">Font Size</label>
        <select id="font-size" name="font-size">
          <option value="small">Small</option>
          <option value="medium" selected>Medium</option>
          <option value="large">Large</option>
        </select>
      </div>
    </fieldset>

    <fieldset>
      <legend>Notification Settings</legend>

      <div class="form-group">
        <input type="checkbox" id="email-notif" name="email-notif" checked>
        <label for="email-notif">Email Notifications</label>
      </div>

      <div class="form-group">
        <input type="checkbox" id="push-notif" name="push-notif" checked>
        <label for="push-notif">Push Notifications</label>
      </div>
    </fieldset>
  </form>
  </main>

  <footer>
    <button class="secondary-button" id="cancel-settings">Cancel</button>
    <button class="primary-button" id="save-settings">Save Changes</button>
  </footer>
  </div>
</div>
```

CHAPTER 2 ARIA

And here is the JavaScript:

```
const openButton = document.getElementById('open-dialog');
const dialog = document.getElementById('settings-dialog');
const closeButton = dialog.querySelector('.close-button');
const cancelButton = document.getElementById('cancel-settings');
const saveButton = document.getElementById('save-settings');

let previouslyFocused;
const focusableElements = dialog.querySelectorAll(
  'button, [href], input, select, textarea, [tabindex]:
  not([tabindex="-1"])'
);
const firstFocusable = focusableElements[0];
const lastFocusable = focusableElements[focusableElements.length - 1];
function openDialog() {
  previouslyFocused = document.activeElement;

  dialog.hidden = false;

  firstFocusable.focus();

  document.body.style.overflow = 'hidden';

  document.addEventListener('keydown', handleEscapeKey);
  dialog.addEventListener('keydown', trapFocus);
}
function closeDialog() {
  dialog.hidden = true;

  previouslyFocused.focus();

  document.body.style.overflow = '';
  document.removeEventListener('keydown', handleEscapeKey);
  dialog.removeEventListener('keydown', trapFocus);
}
```

```
function handleEscapeKey(event) {
  if (event.key === 'Escape') {
    closeDialog();
  }
}
function trapFocus(event) {
  if (event.key === 'Tab') {
    if (event.shiftKey && document.activeElement === firstFocusable) {
      event.preventDefault();
      lastFocusable.focus();
    }
    else if (!event.shiftKey && document.activeElement === lastFocusable) {
      event.preventDefault();
      firstFocusable.focus();
    }
  }
}
openButton.addEventListener('click', openDialog);
closeButton.addEventListener('click', closeDialog);
cancelButton.addEventListener('click', closeDialog);
saveButton.addEventListener('click', () -> {
  closeDialog();
});
dialog.addEventListener('click', (event) => {
  if (event.target === dialog) {
    closeDialog();
  }
});
```

- HTML provides structure with semantic elements.
- ARIA enhances semantics:
    - **role="dialog"** identifies the purpose.
    - **aria-labelledby** connects to a title.
    - **aria-describedby** provides additional context.

- **aria-modal="true"** tells the screen readers that a content-behind dialog is inert.
- JavaScript provides behavior.
    - Focus management (trap focus, restore focus)
    - Keyboard handling (space to close, tab trapping)
    - State management (open/close, attributes)

Here are some best practices for HTML, ARIA, and JavaScript to work harmony:

- Start with right semantic HTML.
- Add ARIA only when needed.
- Keep states synchronized.
- Manage focus.
- Test with assistive technology.

These are common pitfalls to avoid:

- Keyboard traps
- Forgetting to announce dynamic change

```
// INCORRECT: Silent update
function updateResults() {
  resultsContainer.innerHTML = '<p>Found 10 matching items</p>';
}

// CORRECT: Announce the update
function updateResults() {
  resultsContainer.innerHTML = '<p>Found 10 matching items</p>';
  document.getElementById('status').textContent = 'Found 10 matching items';
}
```

- Setting ARIA attributes with invalid values

  ```
  // INCORRECT: Invalid value
  button.setAttribute('aria-expanded', 'yes'); // Should be 'true' or 'false'

  // CORRECT: Valid boolean value as string
  button.setAttribute('aria-expanded', 'true');
  ```

By combining these technologies, you can create interfaces that are not just visually appealing but fully functional for all users, regardless of how they access the Web.

These patterns are reusable. Once you understand them, you can apply them to any component that you build.

Summary and Next Steps

This chapter covered the following essential concepts that will build upon your semantic HTML foundation:

- **Most common ARIA attributes**: The chapter covered the key attributes of ARIA like aria-expanded, aria-hidden, and aria-required and how to use them.

- **Navigation with ARIA and common pitfalls**: You learned how to build accessible navigation and what pitfalls to avoid.

- **Modal implementation**: You learned how to implement modal boxes correctly with ARIA.

With semantic HTML and ARIA in your toolkit, you can now create structural and interactive accessible pages!

Understanding when and how to properly implement ARIA ensures that the pages you build work nicely with assistive technology.

The next chapter will focus on colors and accessibility, exploring how colors and contrast work and ensuring that all users have a great experience on the Web.

CHAPTER 3

Colors and Accessibility

Color is one of the most powerful tools when designing websites and applications. It establishes brand identity, evokes emotional responses, and directs user attention.

For example, a big red "!"can signal that something is important.

A green button often can mean Submit, and light gray text might indicate something is disabled.

For all its beauty and expressive potential, color presents significant accessibility challenges that many developers overlook.

More than 300 million people worldwide have some form of color deficiency. Millions have visual impairments that affect how they perceive brightness and contrast.

Accessible color design is not just about compliance. Color should embody the core principle of the Web, which is universal access to information regardless of ability or circumstances.

Think of your favorite app or website. The colors probably play a big part in why you like it.

In this chapter, you will learn about the critical relationship between colors and accessibility. First we will examine why it's essential to pay close attention to colors and how they affect user interactions.

Then I will explain the Web Content Accessibility Guidelines (WCAG) and how they can help your web applications meet accessibility standards.

Also, it's important to learn about colors used in form validations.

For example, we will talk about how using proper colors can reduce errors and improve overall interaction.

Additionally, you'll learn about how colors work with charts and graphs.

CHAPTER 3   COLORS AND ACCESSIBILITY

Why We Need to Pay Attention to Colors

As mentioned, a significant number of people have some form of color blindness.

For example, if you have multiple colored buttons and you tell the user to click the blue button to toggle the menu, how will the user know that button is blue if they are color blind? To help these users, you need to ensure that color is not the only way of showing information.

There are users with low vision and with contrast needs.

For example, if you have light gray text on a white background, some user will not be able to see the text. Contrasting the text and background colors is essential for these users. Poor color contrast makes text blend into the background.

Also, you need to think about device limitations. Not all users use the newest devices to browse the Web or use applications.

In addition, sunlight can pose a problem.

A quick way to test this out is to view an application in grayscale and see if it still looks good without color.

WCAG

The WCAG provides a comprehensive framework for making web content accessible to people with disabilities.

Within these guidelines, color receives particular attention, both because of anesthetics and because of the functional component of web interface.

WCAG addresses color accessibility through numbered principles.

Use of Color (WCAG 2.1 SC 1.4.1)

You need to provide noncolor cues in addition to color. For example, think about a form field.

Required form fields should not be indicated only by a color highlight. There should be some other sign, like an asterisk or label.

Also, usually developers just use blue for hyperlinks. But you need to set them to be bold or use underline so all users can recognize them as links.

By adding shapes, text, or icons to forms and links, all users can distinguish the information or status being conveyed.

Contrast Ratio for Text (WCAG 2.1 SC 1.4.3)

This is another well-known color requirement. Contrast levels help users with low vision or color vision deficiencies to read content comfortably.

All in all, higher contrast is generally better for readability.

The WCAG defines two levels of conformance:

Level AA:

- Regular text must have a contrast ratio of at least 4:5:1.
- Large text (18pt or 14pt bold and larger) requires a minimum of 3:1.
- UI components need a contrast ratio of at least 3:1 against adjacent colors.

LEVEL AAA:

- Regular text must meet a more stringent 7:1 contrast ratio.
- Large text requires at least 4:5:1.

These ratios are not arbitrary, but they are based on research about human visual perception and minimum threshold needed for various conditions.

Common Pitfalls

One frequent challenge involves maintaining app colors while meeting contrast requirements.

When your corporate color palette includes light or midtone colors, they often fail contrast tests when used for text.

Solution include:

- Darkening application colors for text elements while using original colors for larger decorative elements.
- Creating "accessibility variants" of app colors specifically for text content.

Another challenge concerns hover and focus state that rely solely on color.

Better approaches include:

- Adding underlines or borders/focus/hover
- Implementing slight changes/animations
- Adding focus indicators that combine color with other visual changes

These might seem like big constraints when developing, but they ultimately push designers toward more thoughtful, robust interfaces. By embracing and using these standards, you will create designs and app UIs not only for users with disabilities but for everyone with challenging conditions like bright or poorly calibrated displays.

Colors and Forms

The following is a complete example of form validation that follows the WCAG color accessibility guidelines. It demonstrates both the inaccessible and accessible approaches side-by-side.

HTML:

```html
<!DOCTYPE html>
<html lang="en">
<head>
    <meta charset="UTF-8">
    <meta name="viewport" content="width=device-width, initial-scale=1.0">
    <title>Accessible Form Validation</title>
    <link rel="stylesheet" href="styles.css">
</head>
<body>
    <h1>Form Validation Color Accessibility</h1>

    <fieldset>
        <legend>Inaccessible Approach (Color Only)</legend>
        <p>This form relies solely on color to indicate validation status - problematic for users with color blindness.</p>

        <form class="inaccessible">
            <div class="form-group error">
                <label for="inaccessible-email">Email (Error State)</label>
```

```html
            <input type="email" id="inaccessible-email"
            value="invalid-email">
            <!-- No error text or icon, just red color -->
        </div>

        <div class="form-group success">
            <label for="inaccessible-name">Name (Success State)</label>
            <input type="text" id="inaccessible-name" value="John Doe">
            <!-- No success text or icon, just green color -->
        </div>
    </form>
</fieldset>

<fieldset>
    <legend>Accessible Approach (WCAG Compliant)</legend>
    <p>This form uses multiple visual cues beyond color to indicate
    status.</p>

    <form class="accessible">
        <div class="form-group error">
            <label for="accessible-email">Email (Error State)</label>
            <input type="email" id="accessible-email" value="invalid-
            email" aria-describedby="email-error">
            <div id="email-error" class="feedback-text">
                <span class="icon error-icon" aria-hidden="true">
                </span>
                Please enter a valid email address
            </div>
        </div>

        <div class="form-group success">
            <label for="accessible-name">Name (Success State)</label>
            <input type="text" id="accessible-name" value="John Doe"
            aria-describedby="name-success">
            <div id="name-success" class="feedback-text">
                <span class="icon success-icon" aria-hidden="true">
                </span>
```

CHAPTER 3   COLORS AND ACCESSIBILITY

```
                    Looks good!
                </div>
            </div>

            <button type="submit" class="submit-button">Submit
            Form</button>
        </form>
    </fieldset>

    <fieldset>
        <legend>Text Contrast Examples</legend>

        <div class="contrast-example poor-contrast">
            This text has poor contrast (1.8:1 ratio) and fails WCAG
            standards
        </div>

        <div class="contrast-example good-contrast">
            This text has good contrast (4.5:1 ratio) and meets WCAG AA
            standards
        </div>
    </fieldset>
</body>
</html>
```

CSS:

```
body {
    font-family: system-ui, -apple-system, sans-serif;
    line-height: 1.5;
    max-width: 800px;
    margin: 0 auto;
    padding: 20px;
}

.form-group {
    margin-bottom: 20px;
}
```

```css
label {
    display: block;
    margin-bottom: 5px;
    font-weight: bold;
}
input {
    width: 100%;
    padding: 10px;
    border: 2px solid #ccc;
    border-radius: 4px;
    font-size: 16px;
}
/* Inaccessible validation - color only */
.inaccessible .error input {
    border-color: #ff0000; /* Red border */
}
.inaccessible .success input {
    border-color: #00aa00; /* Green border */
}
/* Accessible validation - with multiple cues */
.accessible .error input {
    border-color: #d32f2f; /* WCAG AA compliant red */
}
.accessible .success input {
    border-color: #2e7d32; /* WCAG AA compliant green */
}
.feedback-text {
    margin-top: 5px;
    font-size: 14px;
}
.accessible .error .feedback-text {
    color: #d32f2f;
    display: flex;
    align-items: center;
}
```

```css
.accessible .success .feedback-text {
    color: #2e7d32;
    display: flex;
    align-items: center;
}
.icon {
    display: inline-block;
    width: 18px;
    height: 18px;
    margin-right: 5px;
    background-repeat: no-repeat;
    background-position: center;
}
.error-icon {
    background-image: url("data:image/svg+xml,%3Csvg xmlns='http://www.
    w3.org/2000/svg' viewBox='0 0 24 24' fill='%23d32f2f'%3E%3Cpath d='M12
    2C6.48 2 2 6.48 2 12s4.48 10 10 10 10-4.48 10-10S17.52 2 12 2zm1
    15h-2v-2h2v2zm0-4h-2V7h2v6z'/%3E%3C/svg%3E");
}
.success-icon {
    background-image: url("data:image/svg+xml,%3Csvg xmlns='http://www.
    w3.org/2000/svg' viewBox='0 0 24 24' fill='%232e7d32'%3E%3Cpath d='M12
    2C6.48 2 2 6.48 2 12s4.48 10 10 10 10-4.48 10-10S17.52 2 12 2zm-2
    15l-5-5 1.41-1.41L10 14.17l7.59-7.59L19 8l-9 9z'/%3E%3C/svg%3E");
}
fieldset {
    border: 1px solid #ddd;
    padding: 20px;
    margin-bottom: 30px;
    border-radius: 4px;
}
legend {
    padding: 0 10px;
    font-weight: bold;
}
```

```css
.contrast-example {
    padding: 10px;
    margin-bottom: 10px;
}
.poor-contrast {
    background-color: #f0f0f0;
    color: #a0a0a0; /* Low contrast - fails WCAG */
}

.good-contrast {
    background-color: #f0f0f0;
    color: #595959; /* Good contrast - passes WCAG AA */
}
.submit-button {
    padding: 10px 15px;
    background-color: #0056b3;
    color: white;
    border: none;
    border-radius: 4px;
    cursor: pointer;
    font-size: 16px;
}
```

Figure 3-1 shows the difference between innaccessible and accessible form validation approaches.

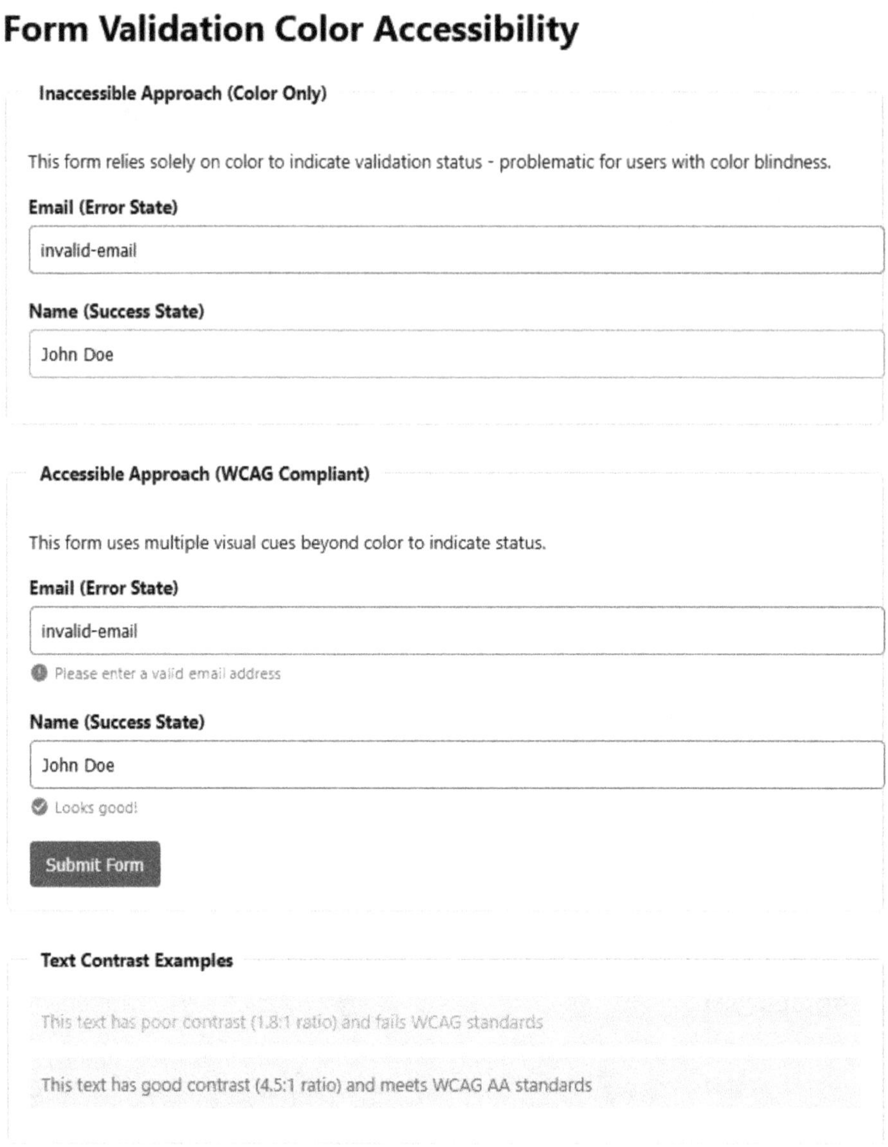

CHAPTER 3 COLORS AND ACCESSIBILITY

Form Validation Color Accessibility

Inaccessible Approach (Color Only)

This form relies solely on color to indicate validation status - problematic for users with color blindness.

Email (Error State)

```
invalid-email
```

Name (Success State)

```
John Doe
```

Accessible Approach (WCAG Compliant)

This form uses multiple visual cues beyond color to indicate status.

Email (Error State)

```
invalid-email
```
⊘ Please enter a valid email address

Name (Success State)

```
John Doe
```
✓ Looks good!

[Submit Form]

Text Contrast Examples

This text has poor contrast (1.8:1 ratio) and fails WCAG standards

This text has good contrast (4.5:1 ratio) and meets WCAG AA standards

Figure 3-1. WCAG-compatible form

Here are the key accessibility improvements:

- **Not relying solely on color:**
  - The accessible version adds icons along with color cues.
  - Text messages explicitly state the validation status.
  - The border thickness provides additional tactile/visual differentiation.

- **WCAG-compliant contrast ratios:**
  - The default red/green colors are replaced with darker variants that maintain sufficient contrast.
  - Text feedback messages use colors that meet the 4.5:1 minimum contrast ratio against white.
- **Semantic improvements:**
  - aria-describedby connects input fields with their validation messages.
  - Error messages are programmatically associated with their inputs.
  - Icons use aria-hidden="true" so screen readers do not announce them redundantly.

  Remember from previous chapter, no ARIA is better than wrongly used ARIA !
- **Multiple sensory channels:**
  - Visual indicators (colors, icons, text)
  - Semantic structure (for assistive technologies)
  - Clear text descriptions that don't rely on the perception of color

Colors and Charts

Data visualizations and charts are fundamentally about communication. When I say communication, I mean transforming raw numbers and relationships into insights that can be quickly grasped and understood.

Yet for many people with disabilities, charts are not completely inaccessible. When you rely only on color to convey critical information, you exclude a significant portion of the audience.

In fields like healthcare, finance, and public policy, misinterpreted data can lead to serious consequences. A physician who is unable to distinguish between red and green trend lines on a patient's chart might miss vital signals. A financial analyst with deuteranopia reviewing color-coded market performance data might make decisions based on incomplete information.

Before implementing solutions, you must understand the various ways people perceive color. Color vision deficiencies take several forms:

Protanopia/protanomaly: Reduced sensitivity to red light, making reds appear darker and less distinct from greens

Deuteranopia/deuteranomaly: The most common form of color blindness, affecting green perception and making red and green difficult to distinguish

Tritanopia/tritanomaly: Rare blue-yellow color blindness, complicating distinctions between blue and green, and yellow and violet

Achromatopsia: Complete color blindness, where all colors are perceived as shades of gray

Each type presents unique challenges for data visualization. Red-green contrasts—commonly used to indicate positive/negative values or to highlight deviations—become particularly problematic since these are precisely the colors most affected by the most common forms of color vision deficiencies (CVD).

The cornerstone of accessible chart design is redundant encoding, meaning using multiple visual properties to convey the same information:

Patterns and textures: Apply distinctive patterns (stripes, dots, cross hatches) to different data series so they remain distinguishable even in grayscale.

Shapes and markers: In line charts and scatter plots, use distinct shapes for data points (circles, squares, triangles) rather than relying on color alone.

Direct labeling: Place labels directly on chart elements rather than requiring users to match colors to a separate legend.

Border differentiation: Add contrasting borders around elements to enhance their distinctiveness.

Choosing appropriate colors dramatically affects accessibility:

High-contrast palettes: Ensure sufficient contrast between colors, particularly for adjacent elements.

ColorBrewer scales: Utilize scientifically designed color scales specifically created for data visualization, many of which are CVD-friendly.

Blue-orange instead of red-green: Replace problematic red-green contrasts with blue-orange palettes that remain distinguishable for most forms of color blindness.

Varying luminance: Create palettes with varying brightness levels, not just hue differences.

Some of implementation technologies with web technologies include combining SVG and ARIA.

```
<svg role="img" aria-labelledby="chart-title chart-desc">
  <title id="chart-title">Quarterly Sales by Region (2024)</title>
  <desc id="chart-desc">Bar chart showing sales performance across four
  regions, with the Northeast leading in Q3.</desc>
  <!-- Chart elements go here -->
</svg>
```

The following are key ARIA attributes for chart elements:

- `role="img"` for the chart container
- `aria-labelledby` to connect the chart with its title and description
- `role="graphics-symbol"` or `role="graphics-document"` for chart elements
- `aria-label` for individual data points or segments

Charts and Examples

You also need to think about the different type of charts and which ones to use.

The following are some examples:

- **Line chart**

    Problem: Multiple lines distinguished only by color become indistinguishable for users with CVD.

Solutions:

- Use distinctive line patterns (solid, dashed, dotted).
- Employ different markers for data points (circle, square, triangle).
- Use direct labeling at line endpoints.
- Vary the line thickness in addition to color.

Bar charts

Problem: Multiple bar categories distinguished only by color.

Solutions:

- Apply patterns or textures to bars.
- Use consistent positioning (e.g., Product A always leftmost in each group).
- Add direct value labels.
- Provide strong borders between adjacent bars.

- **Pie/donut charts**

  Problem: Segments distinguished only by color; difficult to compare values.

  Solutions:

  - Apply distinctive patterns to segments.
  - Add direct percentage labels.
  - Use clear borders between segments.
  - Consider alternatives like bar charts for complex comparisons.
  - Limit to five to six segments maximum.

- Heat maps

  Problem: Data values mapped solely to color intensity.

  Solutions:

  - Use patterns combined with color.
  - Add numeric labels in cells.

CHAPTER 3   COLORS AND ACCESSIBILITY

- Choose color scales carefully (blue to orange rather than red to green).
- Provide interactive tool tips with precise values.

You need to test all of this while you are building and after you finish. The following are some testing tools:

Colorblindly: Browser extension that simulates various types of color blindness

Sim Daltonism: macOS application for color blindness simulation

Adobe Photoshop's color blindness proofing: Professional tool for designers

Contrast Analyzers

These are analyzers:

- **WebAIM Contrast Checker**: Verifies contrast ratios between chart elements
- **Colour Contrast Analyser**: Desktop application for detailed analysis

Screen Reader Testing

These are screen reader testers:

- Test chart navigation and information conveyance with NVDA, JAWS, or VoiceOver
- Ensures all data points are properly announced
- Verifies that relationships between data are clear

The gold standard remains testing with actual users who have diverse visual abilities:

- Include users with various forms of color blindness.
- Test with screen reader users.
- Gather feedback on clarity and comprehensibility.

The Future

The field of accessible data visualization continues to evolve with these emerging technologies:

> **Sonification**: Converting data trends into audio patterns, enabling auditory chart perception
>
> **Haptic feedback**: Using tactile feedback to represent data patterns in interactive visualizations
>
> **AI-assisted alt text**: Automated generation of detailed chart descriptions for screen readers
>
> **Personalized visualizations**: Adapting chart colors and features to individual user preferences and needs
>
> **WebXR and spatial visualizations**: Creating multisensory data experiences that don't rely solely on vision

Using colors for accessibility and data visualizations is not merely about compliance but universal design that improves the experience for everyone.

As you implement the techniques in this chapter, remember that accessibility visualization is not about removing colors; it's about using colors intentionally, alongside other visual properties.

When you design with accessibility in mind from the start, you don't just accommodate differences. You create better visualizations for all users.

Summary and Next Steps

The following are the key concepts that extend your semantic HTML and ARIA knowledge:

- **WCAG Guidelines**: You now understand how WCAG guidelines address colors, contrast, and visual accessibility requirements.
- **Building accessible forms**: You learned how to build accessible forms and what to pay attention to when building them.

– **Common pitfalls:** You learned about pitfalls like animations, borders, and colors that you need to use and pay attention to.

– **Accessible charts:** You learned how to create accessible line charts, bar charts, heat maps, and pie/donut charts, and what tools to use to test them

The next chapter will teach you how to use accessible images that are meaningful to users with alt text, image text, and more!

CHAPTER 4

Accessible Images

Images enrich our digital experience. They convey emotions, information, and context in a way that text often cannot. Images engage users visually.

The concept of "accessible images" may seem a little paradoxical. However, images can become barrier for the users with visual impairment.

Ensuring the images are accessible means providing nice, fair, and impartial experiences for everyone, regardless of their abilities.

This involves understanding how users with disabilities need to interact with images and implementing techniques like alt text, ARIA attributes, descriptive captions, and appropriate markup.

In this chapter, we will explore the fundamentals of image accessibility, examining the best practices for writing effective alternate text, understanding when to use decorative images, and exploring techniques to ensure your visuals support all users.

By the end of chapter, you will be equipped with practical strategies to implement image accessibility.

Importance of Alt Text

Alternative text, more commonly known as *alt text*, is a description of the image (brief description) that conveys meaning to individuals who use screen readers or have images disabled in their browsers.

Well-written alt text improves accessibility by providing the necessary context and information that an image would provide visually. It ensures that all users, including those with visual impairments, cognitive limitations, or even low bandwidth or slower Internet speed, have equal access to information on your website/application.

I'll show you examples of poorly written and well-written alt text

CHAPTER 4   ACCESSIBLE IMAGES

Poorly Written Alt Text

The following alt text is too vague:

- **Image:** A professional photograph of medical team performing a surgery
- **Bad alt text**: "Doctors"

This alt text fails to convey information for the users who can't see the image. The following alt text is redundant:

- **Image:** A chart show rising sales figures for 2024
- **Bad alt text**: "Chart image"

This alt text says only that the image is a chart; it completely omits what is on the chart.

The following example is overloaded with unnecessary details:

- **Image:** The woman at a café
- **Poor alt text:** "Female with red hair in blue T-shirt at a green table holding a red ceramic mug with her right hand in a café with large windows and plants on the windy day"

This alt text drowns out the essential information with excessive details that are not relevant to the image's purpose.

Well-Written Alt Text

The following alt text is contextually relevant:

- **Image:** A professional photograph of medical team performing a surgery
- **Good alt text:** "Surgical team of four medical professionals performing a heart transplant operation"

This alt text clearly identifies what's happening and provides context that matters.

The following alt text conveys information about the data.

- **Image:** A chart show rising sales figures for 2024
- **Good alt text:** "Bar chart showing quarterly sales growth of 15% in Q1, 23% in Q2 and 33% in Q3 of 2024."

The alt text focuses on the data itself, in other words, the actual information that is meant to be conveyed.

The following alt text is balanced and purposeful:

Image: The woman at a café

Good alt text: "Woman enjoying coffee while working on her laptop at a sunny café"

This version capture the point of the image without getting lost in irrelevant information.

More Tips for Writing Good Alt Text

When writing alt text, think about why the image exists within the content and what information it conveys. For example, the same image may have different alt text depending on context.

Also, do not write "image of" or "picture of" in alt text. Screen readers already read that's it's the image.

I suggest not writing more than 125 characters of alt text. You should focus on essential information only.

Further, if image is merely decorative, you can set empty alt="" text so screen readers will skip it entirely.

There also functional images, like icons, for example, such as print icons.

Here is the bad example of the alt text for a functional image/icon:

```
<a href="/print"><img src="print-icon.png" alt="printer icon "></a>
```

Here is a good version:

```
<a href="/print"><img src="print-icon.png" alt="Print"></a>
```

CHAPTER 4   ACCESSIBLE IMAGES

Accessibility Standards for Images: WCAG and POUR

Multiple accessibility standards and guidelines address how to handle images. The most important are the Web Content Accessibility Guidelines (WCAG) and Accessible Rich Internet Applications (ARIA).

In this chapter, we will focus on WCAG 2.1 (3.0 is out, but it will need couple years until it becomes standard).

The following are the key success criteria for images (**https://www.w3.org/TR/ UNDERSTANDING-WCAG20/intro.html**). These four fundamental principles are often referred by the acronym POUR.

1. **Perceivable**: Information and user interface components must be presentable to users in ways they can perceive.

   This means users must be able to perceive the information being presented (it can't be invisible to all of their senses).

2. **Operable**: User interface components and navigation must be operable.

   This means users must be able to operate the interface (the interface cannot require interactions that a user cannot perform).

3. **Understandable**: The information and the operation of user interface must be understandable.

   This means users must be able to understand the information as well as the operation of the user interface (the content or operation cannot be beyond their understanding).

4. **Robust**: The content must be robust enough that it can be interpreted reliably by a wide variety of user agents, including assistive technologies.

   This means users must be able to access the content as technologies advance (as technologies and user agents evolve, the content should remain accessible).

Conformance Levels and Techniques for Meeting Image Requirements

WCAG 2.1 defines three levels of conformance:

- **Level A:** The most basic level of accessibility. Meeting these criteria is essential as they address barriers that would completely prevent certain groups from accessing content.

- **Level AA:** The target level for most websites. It addresses significant barriers and is referenced in most legislation worldwide.

- **Level AAA:** The highest level of accessibility, addressing subtle and specialized accessibility concerns.

Most organizations aim for Level AA compliance, which encompasses all Level A criteria plus additional requirements.

H2: Combining adjacent image and text links for the same resource

H24: Providing text alternatives for the `area` elements of image maps

H30: Providing link text that describes the purpose of a link for anchor elements

H35: Providing text alternatives on `applet` elements

H36: Using `alt` attributes on `input` elements of type "image"

H37: Using `alt` attributes on `img` elements

H45: Using `longdesc`

H46: Using `noembed` with `embed`

H53: Using the body of the `object` element

H67: Using `alt` text that is null on images used for decoration

Level AA encompasses these ARIA techniques:

- **ARIA6:** Using `aria-label` to provide labels for objects
- **ARIA9:** Using `aria-labelledby` to concatenate a label from several text nodes

- **ARIA10:** Using `aria-labelledby` to provide a text alternative for non-text content

- **ARIA15:** Using `aria-describedby` to provide descriptions of image

In general, you do not need ARIA attributes for images. The native element is enough. As you know from the previous chapter, ARIA comes into the play when not using the <img> tag. For example, use them when using <div>.

Essentially, `role="img"` lets you programmatically designate something as a graphic, and `aria-label="..."` can act like alt text in that scenario.

Also, you need to test the page for WCAG 2.1 compliance.

Specifically, you need to check for the presence of **alt** attributes. Also, pay attention to the **alt text quality**. Testing with screen readers is also important to ensure the content is properly read.

Types of Images and What to Look For

The following are types of images.

Informative

What makes an image informative? An informative image is the image that provides content that is not made redundant by the surrounding text. Examples are product photos, maps, location images, informational info graphics, charts, diagrams, and graphs.

Let's look at an e-commerce product as an example.

(Each image in an e-commerce store needs to have alt text. Many content managements tools provide this out of the box.)

Here is example of well-written alt text for a product:

```
<img src="headphones.jpg" alt="Wireless over-ear headphones in matte black with noise cancellation">
```

Decorative

Decorative images are visual elements that serve an aesthetic purpose rather than providing information.

As you learned, images can have an empty alt tag when they are decorative.

Decorative images do the following:

- Add visual appeal without conveying information
- Don't contribute to the understanding of the content
- Could be removed without affecting the page
- Might repeat information that is already in the text
- Are often used for layout, aesthetics, etc.

The following are common types of decorative images:

- Visual styling elements

    ```
    <!-- Dividers, separators, or borders -->
    <img src="fancy-line.png" alt="" />
    <!-- Background textures or patterns -->
    <img src="subtle-pattern.jpg" alt="" />
    <!-- Decorative corners, flourishes, or embellishments -->
    <img src="corner-flourish.png" alt="" />
    ```

- Atmospheric or mood images

    ```
    <!-- Generic stock photos that don't add specific information -->
    <img src-"happy office-workers.jpg" alt="" />

    <!-- Abstract or artistic elements -->
    <img src="abstract-shapes.png" alt="" />
    ```

- Purely decorative images

    ```
    <!-- Decorative illustrations that complement but don't add information -->
    <img src="decorative-leaves.png" alt="" />
    ```

    But also, use CSS when possible for this.

Before marking an image as decorative, ask yourself:

- Would a blind person miss information if there is no image?
- Does the image provide emotion or context?

If you answer "yes" to any of these questions, the image is probably informative and needs proper alt text.

But pay attention. What if you omit alt in an <img> tag, like this:

```
<img src="line.png">
<img src="line.png" alt="">
```

Missing content for the alt tag is incorrect. Screen readers will still read the filename when you set alt to be empty.

Functional

Functional images serve a purpose to control interactive elements on a page. Unlike decorative and informative, functional images perform an action when activated.

Functional images do the following:

- Initiate some action when clicked/tapped
- Function as buttons, controls, links, etc.
- Require user interaction to fulfill their purpose

Imagine you have a shopping cart. You need to describe its function with alt, not its appearance.

```
<!-- Good: Describes function -->
<a href="shopping-cart.html">
  <img src="cart-icon.png" alt="View shopping cart">
</a>

<!-- Not good: Describes appearance -->
<a href="shopping-cart.html">
  <img src="cart-icon.png" alt="Shopping cart icon">
</a>
```

As another example, say you have some kind of video/music player:

```
<button class="play-button">
  <img src="play-button.png" alt="Play video">
</button>
```

```
<button class="volume-icon">
  <img src="volume-icon.png" alt="Mute audio">
</button>

<button class="transcript" aria-expanded="false" aria-controls=
"transcript-panel">
  <img src="expand-icon.png" alt="Show transcript">
</button>
```

By clicking each of these buttons, the video player should trigger the correct information because you have the correct alt text for it.

The first button will be announced redundantly, while the second button will provide a clean, single announcement that clearly describes the button function without repetition.

```
<!-- not good: Redundant alt text -->
  <button>
    <img src="save-icon.png" alt="Save"> Save
  </button>

<!-- correct: Empty alt, letting text speak -->
  <button>
    <img src="save-icon.png" alt=""> Save
  </button>
```

Images of Text

Images of text are used when textual content occurs as an image instead of using actual HTML text.

Text images are the following:

- Logo text
- Text in banners or headers rendered as images
- Image-based buttons with text labels
- Infographics containing textual information
- Screenshots containing text
- Text embedded in photographs (like signs in an image)

These are some good practices when using images of text:

```html
<!-- good: Uses exact text -->
<img src="welcome-banner.png" alt="Welcome to Mountain View Resort">

<!-- Not good: Describes the image instead of providing the text -->
<img src="welcome-banner.png" alt="Banner with welcome message">
```

As you can see, you need to use the same text instead of a banner description.

For infographics, you usually need both alt text and the image.

```html
<img src="cat-journey-infographic.png"
    alt="Cat Journey Map: Awareness of Cats"
    aria-describedby="infographic-description">

<div id="infographic-description" >
  Some detailed infographic..
  1. Text 1
  2. Text 2
  3. etc
</div>
```

When possible, always add text instead of images. In fact, the best solution is to avoid images of text altogether.

```html
<!-- BETTER APPROACH: Using styled HTML text -->
<h1 class="welcome-header">Welcome to Cats garden</h1>
```

You can achieve nice typography with modern HTML, CSS, and JavaScript without adding images.

The WCAG requirements for images of text are as follows:

- Level AA requires that images of text are only used for decoration or where the specific presentation is essential (like logos).

- Text should have a contrast ratio of at least 4.5:1 against its background.

- Text should be resizable without a loss of content or functionality.

Groups of Images

Group images are images used together to present some piece of information.

Groups of images are used for the following:

- Rating stars
- Before/after image comparisons
- Social media share icons
- Related images that tell a story

Rating stars are one of most common types:

```
<!-- Star rating system -->
  <div class="product-rating" aria-label="Product rated 4 out of 5 stars">
    <img src="star-filled.png" alt="">
    <img src="star-filled.png" alt="">
    <img src="star-filled.png" alt="">
    <img src="star-filled.png" alt="">
    <img src="star-empty.png" alt="">
    <span class="rating-text">4.0 out of 5 stars (150reviews)</span>
  </div>
```

To test images, use the screen reader navigation. Ensure that the relationship between images is clear when navigating with a screen reader.

Also keep on mind the keyboard navigation/focus order.

Check that a screen reader user gets both the overall context and the individual image details.

Check also role verification, and test that the ARIA roles are implemented correctly and provide the expected information.

Image Maps

Image maps allow multiple clickable regions within a single image, each linked to a different destination.

CHAPTER 4   ACCESSIBLE IMAGES

Here is an example:

```html
<!-- Accessible client-side image map -->
<img src="office-floorplan.png" alt="Office building floorplan" usemap="#floorplan">

<map name="floorplan">
  <area shape="rect" coords="0,0,100,100" href="reception.html"
  alt="Reception area">
  <area shape="rect" coords="120,0,200,100" href="offices.html"
  alt="Executive offices">
  <area shape="circle" coords="300,50,30" href="conference.html"
  alt="Conference room">
  <area shape="poly" coords="400,10,450,10,450,90,400,90" href="kitchen.
  html" alt="Kitchen and break room">
```

Here is an example of diagrams:

```html
<img src="smartphone-features.jpg" alt="Smartphone features overview
diagram" usemap="#phone-features">

<map name="phone-features">
  <area shape="rect" coords="10,10,80,40" href="camera.html" alt="Triple-
  lens 48MP camera system">
  <area shape="rect" coords="90,10,160,40" href="screen.html" alt="6.5-inch
  OLED display">
  <area shape="rect" coords="10,50,80,80" href="battery.html" alt="5000mAh
  all-day battery">
  <area shape="rect" coords="90,50,160,80" href="processor.html" alt="A15
  Bionic processor">
  <area shape="circle" coords="85,120,20" href="home-button.html"
  alt="Fingerprint sensor and home button">
```

The Web Content Accessibility Guidelines (WCAG) have specific requirements:

- **Client-side only**: Use only client-side image maps (WCAG 2.1 Success Criterion 1.1.1).

- **Complete alt text**: Provide text alternatives for both the image and all area elements (WCAG 2.1 Success Criterion 1.1.1).

- **Keyboard accessibility**: Ensure all areas can be navigated using a keyboard (WCAG 2.1 Success Criterion 2.1.1).

- **Focus indication**: Provide visible focus indicators (WCAG 2.1 Success Criterion 2.4.7).

But pay attention to mistakes; they always happen!

```
<!-- not good: Missing alt attributes -->
<map name="product-map">
   <area shape="rect" coords="10,10,100,50" href="feature1.html">
   <area shape="rect" coords="110,10,200,50" href="feature2.html">

  <!-- good: All areas have alt attributes -->
  <map name="product-map">
    <area shape="rect" coords="10,10,100,50" href="feature1.html"
    alt="Cloud storage feature">
    <area shape="rect" coords="110,10,200,50" href="feature2.html"
    alt="Collaboration tools">
```

In many cases, modern web technologies provide better alternatives to traditional maps. For example, you can use an HTML/CSS approach or modern interactive components (using JavaScript frameworks).

Alt Decision Tree

An alt decision tree is a systematic approach to determine the appropriate alt text for images.

Figure 4-1 can help you learn how to use alt text.

CHAPTER 4 ACCESSIBLE IMAGES

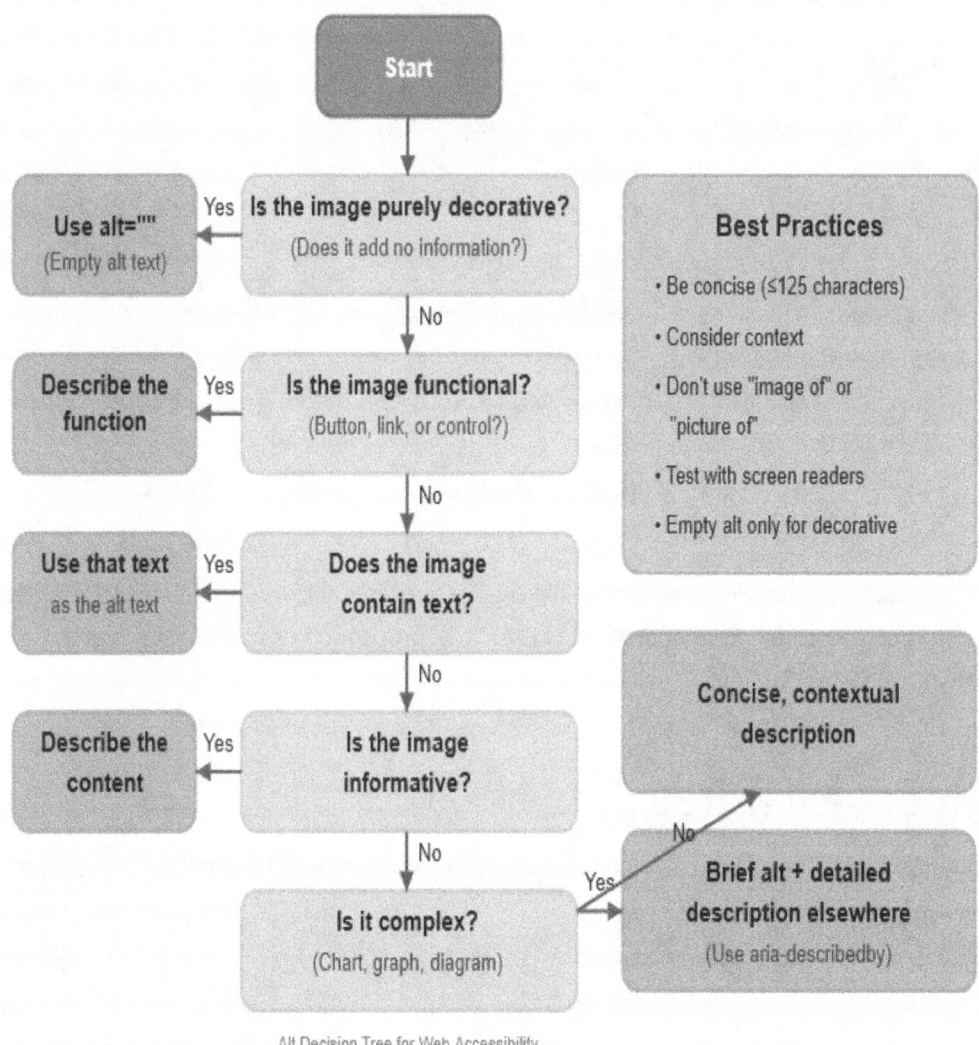

Figure 4-1. Alt decision tree for web accessibility

Summary and Next Steps

This chapter built nicely on previous chapters. These are the key takeaways:

- **Importance of alt text:** You learned why and how good alt text is important in an image tag.

- **WCAG and "POUR":** You learned what is POUR is and why it's important.

- **Type of images:** You learned what types of images exist.

- **ALT decision tree:** You looked at an important diagram that ties everything together.

In the following chapter, you will learn how to use videos and audios with accessibility.

CHAPTER 5

Accessible Videos and Audio

The Web has evolved into a beautiful rich multimedia environment. Video and audio play a central role how we communicate, entertain, educate, etc. Audio and video have become fundamental to the digital experience. But this media landscape can present significant barriers for users with disabilities.

When you create video and audio content, you need to ensure that everyone can participate in our increasingly connected world. When we consider that many people live with some form of disability, it's important to think about accessibility.

Users who are deaf or have bad hearing need captions to access audio content. Those who are blind or have low vision rely on the audio descriptions to understand visual elements.

The good news is that modern technology provides a powerful tool for accessibility features. HTML5 native audio and video elements come with built-in accessibility hooks, CSS can enhance the presentation of media controls, and JavaScript enables us to create custom players.

The challenge is not in technology; you need to understand how to leverage these technologies.

In this chapter, you will see some practical implementations of these tools. You will explore how to properly structure elements such as keyboard navigation, screen readers, subtitles, and more.

Captions and Screen Readers

The foundation of the accessible multimedia lies in a simple but crucial principle: all audio must have text alternatives. Captions represent synchronized text that accompanies audio content, providing not just spoken dialogue but also musical cues and atmospheric audio that contributes to understanding.

This requirement is not just a recommendation; it is a legal requirement so that digital content remains accessible to everyone.

The technical implementation of captions involves precise synchronization between the text and audio timelines. Unlike transcripts, captions need to appear and disappear at precise times to maintain the rhythm with spoken content.

Let's dive to some code!

Here is the HTML of the first example:

```
<video controls preload="metadata" width="640" height="360">
    <source src="presentation.mp4" type="video/mp4">
    <source src="presentation.webm" type="video/webm">

    <!-- Here we put track for different languges -->
    <track kind="captions"
           src="captions-en.vtt"
           srclang="en"
           label="English Captions"
           default>

    <track kind="captions"
           src="captions-es.vtt"
           srclang="es"
           label="Spanish Captions">

    <!-- Fallback content -->
    <p>Your browser doesn't support HTML5 video.
        <a href="presentation.mp4">Download the video</a> instead.</p>
```

As you know, src is short for source; it is the path to the file. The type attribute is the kind of video it is.

And in track we put captions.

The following is an example of a VTT file.

> **Note** Captions for "Beginner Guitar: Learning Your First Chord" tutorial video

```
1
00:00:00.000 --> 00:00:03.200
Hi everyone, I'm Pavle, and welcome back
to Guitar Basics.

2
00:00:03.200 --> 00:00:06.500
Today we're going to learn the G major chord,
one of the most important chords for beginners.

3
00:00:06.500 --> 00:00:08.800
[acoustic guitar being picked up]

4
00:00:08.800 --> 00:00:12.100
First, let's hear how a G major chord
should sound when played correctly.

5
00:00:12.100 --> 00:00:14.300
[clean G major chord strummed - bright, full sound]

6
00:00:14.300 --> 00:00:17.800
Beautiful! Now let's break down
the finger placement step by step.

7
00:00:17.800 --> 00:00:21.200
Place your middle finger on the third fret
of the low E string.

8
00:00:21.200 --> 00:00:23.500
[single note played - low, resonant tone]
```

CHAPTER 5   ACCESSIBLE VIDEOS AND AUDIO

```
9
00:00:23.500 --> 00:00:27.100
Next, put your ring finger on the third fret
of the high E string.

10
00:00:27.100 --> 00:00:29.400
[single note played - higher pitch]

11
00:00:29.400 --> 00:00:32.800
Finally, place your pinky on the third fret
of the B string.

12
00:00:32.800 --> 00:00:34.900
[single note played - mid-range tone]

13
00:00:34.900 --> 00:00:37.500
Now let's try strumming all six strings together.

14
00:00:37.500 --> 00:00:40.200
[slow downward strum - full G chord ringing]

15
00:00:40.200 --> 00:00:43.600
Great! If any strings sound muted or buzzy,
adjust your finger pressure.
```

Notice how the WebVTT format includes several accessibility features:

- **Precise timing:** Each caption has exact start and end times (00:00:00.000 format).
- **Speaker identification:** "I'm Pavle Paunovic" identifies the speaker.

– **Sound description:** The description "[upbeat music begins], [mouse clicking]" provides context for nonspeech audio.
– **Natural reading rhythm:** The caption duration allows for a comfortable reading speed.

Here is the CSS for captions:

```css
video::cue {
    background-color: rgba(0, 0, 0, 0.8);
    color: white;
    font-family: Arial, sans-serif;
    font-size: 18px;
    line-height: 1.4;
    padding: 0.2em 0.5em;
    border-radius: 4px;
}

/* Style for sound effect descriptions */
video::cue(.sound-effect) {
    color: #ffff99;
    font-style: italic;
}

/* Style for speaker identification */
video::cue(.speaker) {
    color: #87ceeb;
    font-weight: bold;
}
```

– Figure 5-1 and Figure 5-2 show how the video would look.

CHAPTER 5   ACCESSIBLE VIDEOS AND AUDIO

Figure 5-1. *Captions for beginning guitar, introduction, and theme of the video*

Figure 5-2. *Example of sound description*

CHAPTER 5   ACCESSIBLE VIDEOS AND AUDIO

As you can see in Figure 5-3, you can choose what language you want to be used in the HTML.

Figure 5-3. *Choosing language and controls*

You have now seen a basic example of video and transcription.

Let's see an example of screen reader compatibility. You need to ensure that media player controls and text alternatives are accessible to screen readers. For example, the play/pause buttons should be announced clearly.

If you are using a <button> element with visible text like Play, it will be accessible by default. If the control is an icon with visible text, you should add aria-label="Play" or include off-screen text so screen readers can identify it. When the state toggles (play versus pause), update the label or use a toggle state like aria-pressed. Additionally, some advanced media players use live regions to announce captions or important status changes to screen readers.

Basic Accessible Media Controls

But what if you want to create accessible buttons and controls for users?

You can create custom buttons with ARIA attributes, as shown here:

```
<div class="media-player" role="region" aria-label="Video player">
    <video id="mainVideo" controls width="1024" height="640">
```

```html
      <source src="tutorial.mp4" type="video/mp4">
      <track kind="captions" src="captions-en.vtt" srclang="en"
      label="English" default>
      <p>Your browser doesn't support HTML5 video. <a href="tutorial.
      mp4">Download instead</a>.</p>

  <!-- Custom accessible controls -->
  <div class="player-controls" role="toolbar" aria-label="Video
  controls">
    <button id="playPauseBtn"
            class="control-btn"
            aria-label="Play video"
            aria-pressed="false">
      <span class="icon play-icon" aria-hidden="true"> </span>
      <span class="sr-only">Play</span>
    </button>

    <button id="muteBtn"
            class="control-btn"
            aria-label="Mute audio"
            aria-pressed="false">
      <span class="icon volume-icon" aria-hidden="true"> </span>
      <span class="sr-only">Mute</span>
    </button>

    <div class="volume-control">
      <label for="volumeSlider" class="sr-only">Volume</label>
      <input type="range"
             id="volumeSlider"
             min="0"
             max="100"
             value="50"
             aria-label="Volume control"
             aria-valuetext="Volume at 50 percent">
    </div>
```

```
        <button id="captionsBtn"
                class="control-btn"
                aria-label="Toggle captions"
                aria-pressed="true">
          <span class="icon cc-icon" aria-hidden="true">CC</span>
          <span class="sr-only">Captions on</span>
        </button>

        <div class="time-display" aria-live="polite" aria-atomic="true">
          <span id="currentTime">0:00</span> / <span
            id="duration">0:00</span>
        </div>
      </div>

      <!-- Live region for caption announcements (for deaf-blind
      users) -->
      <div id="captionLiveRegion"
           class="sr-only"
           aria-live="assertive"
           aria-atomic="false"></div>

      <!-- Status announcements -->
      <div id-"statusRegion"
           class="sr-only"
           aria-live="polite"
           aria-atomic="true"></div>
    </div>
```

Here is the CSS:

```
/* Hide content visually but keep it available to screen readers */
.sr-only {
  position: absolute;
  width: 1px;
  height: 1px;
  padding: 0;
  margin: -1px;
  overflow: hidden;
```

```css
  clip: rect(0, 0, 0, 0);
  white-space: nowrap;
  border: 0;
}

/* Ensure focus indicators are visible */
.control-btn:focus {
  outline: 2px solid #007cba;
  outline-offset: 2px;
}

/* Style for pressed state indicators */
.control-btn[aria-pressed="true"] {
  background-color: #007cba;
  color: white;
}
```

Here is the JavaScript for dynamic controls:

```js
class AccessibleVideoPlayer {
  constructor(videoElement) {
    this.video = videoElement;
    this.playPauseBtn = document.getElementById('playPauseBtn');
    this.muteBtn = document.getElementById('muteBtn');
    this.captionsBtn = document.getElementById('captionsBtn');
    this.volumeSlider = document.getElementById('volumeSlider');
    this.captionLiveRegion = document.getElementById('captionLiveRegion');
    this.statusRegion = document.getElementById('statusRegion');

    this.initializeControls();
    this.initializeCaptions();
  }

  initializeControls() {
    // Play/Pause button with state management
    this.playPauseBtn.addEventListener('click', () => {
      if (this.video.paused) {
        this.video.play();
```

```
      this.updatePlayPauseButton('pause');
      this.announceStatus('Video playing');
    } else {
      this.video.pause();
      this.updatePlayPauseButton('play');
      this.announceStatus('Video paused');
    }
  });

  // Mute button with state management
  this.muteBtn.addEventListener('click', () => {
    this.video.muted = !this.video.muted;
    this.updateMuteButton();
  });

  // Volume slider with live feedback
  this.volumeSlider.addEventListener('input', (e) => {
    const volume = e.target.value / 100;
    this.video.volume = volume;
    e.target.setAttribute('aria-valuetext', `Volume at ${e.target.value}
    percent`);
  });

  // Caption toggle
  this.captionsBtn.addEventListener('click', () => {
    this.toggleCaptions();
  });

  // Time updates
  this.video.addEventListener('timeupdate', () => {
    this.updateTimeDisplay();
  });

  // Keyboard navigation
  this.video.addEventListener('keydown', (e) => {
    this.handleKeyboardControls(e);
  });
}
```

CHAPTER 5   ACCESSIBLE VIDEOS AND AUDIO

```
updatePlayPauseButton(state) {
  const isPlaying = state === 'pause';
  const icon = this.playPauseBtn.querySelector('.icon');
  const srText = this.playPauseBtn.querySelector('.sr-only');

  if (isPlaying) {
    this.playPauseBtn.setAttribute('aria-label', 'Pause video');
    this.playPauseBtn.setAttribute('aria-pressed', 'true');
    icon.textContent = '⏸';

    srText.textContent = 'Pause';
  } else {
    this.playPauseBtn.setAttribute('aria-label', 'Play video');
    this.playPauseBtn.setAttribute('aria-pressed', 'false');
    icon.textContent = '▶';

    srText.textContent = 'Play';
  }
}

updateMuteButton() {
  const icon = this.muteBtn.querySelector('.icon');
  const srText = this.muteBtn.querySelector('.sr-only');

  if (this.video.muted) {
    this.muteBtn.setAttribute('aria-label', 'Unmute audio');
    this.muteBtn.setAttribute('aria-pressed', 'true');
    icon.textContent = '🔇';

    srText.textContent = 'Unmute';
    this.announceStatus('Audio muted');
  } else {
    this.muteBtn.setAttribute('aria-label', 'Mute audio');
    this.muteBtn.setAttribute('aria-pressed', 'false');
    icon.textContent = '🔊';

    srText.textContent = 'Mute';
    this.announceStatus('Audio unmuted');
  }
}
```

```
toggleCaptions() {
  const track = this.video.textTracks[0];
  const isEnabled = track.mode === 'showing';

  if (isEnabled) {
    track.mode = 'hidden';
    this.captionsBtn.setAttribute('aria-pressed', 'false');
    this.captionsBtn.querySelector('.sr-only').textContent =
    'Captions off';
    this.announceStatus('Captions disabled');
  } else {
    track.mode = 'showing';
    this.captionsBtn.setAttribute('aria-pressed', 'true');
    this.captionsBtn.querySelector('.sr-only').textContent = 'Captions on';
    this.announceStatus('Captions enabled');
  }
}

// Live region for caption text (primarily for deaf-blind users)
initializeCaptions() {
  const track = this.video.textTracks[0];
  if (track) {
    track.addEventListener('cuechange', () => {
      const activeCue = track.activeCues[0];
      if (activeCue && this.shouldAnnounceCaptions()) {
        // Only announce captions for users who need them read aloud
        this.captionLiveRegion.textContent = activeCue.text;
      }
    });
  }
}

shouldAnnounceCaptions() {
  // This could be a user preference setting
  // Most blind users prefer audio content over caption announcements
  return localStorage.getItem('announceCaption') === 'true';
}
```

```javascript
updateTimeDisplay() {
  const currentTime = this.formatTime(this.video.currentTime);
  const duration = this.formatTime(this.video.duration);

  document.getElementById('currentTime').textContent = currentTime;
  document.getElementById('duration').textContent = duration;
}

formatTime(seconds) {
  const mins = Math.floor(seconds / 60);
  const secs = Math.floor(seconds % 60);
  return `${mins}:${secs.toString().padStart(2, '0')}`;
}

handleKeyboardControls(e) {
  switch(e.key) {
    case ' ':
      e.preventDefault();
      this.playPauseBtn.click();
      break;
    case 'm':
      this.muteBtn.click();
      break;
    case 'c':
      this.captionsBtn.click();
      break;
    case 'ArrowLeft':
      this.video.currentTime -= 10;
      this.announceStatus(`Rewound 10 seconds to ${this.formatTime(this.video.currentTime)}`);
      break;
    case 'ArrowRight':
      this.video.currentTime += 10;
      this.announceStatus(`Fast forwarded 10 seconds to ${this.formatTime(this.video.currentTime)}`);
```

```
        break;
    }
  }

  announceStatus(message) {
    this.statusRegion.textContent = message;
    // Clear after announcement to avoid repetition
    setTimeout(() => {
      this.statusRegion.textContent = '';
    }, 1000);
  }
}

// Initialize the accessible player
document.addEventListener('DOMContentLoaded', () => {
  const video = document.getElementById('mainVideo');
  new AccessibleVideoPlayer(video);
});
```

You are implementing the following here:

1. **Dynamic ARIA updates:** Button labels and state changes based on the current video state

2. **Live regions:** Status announcements and optional caption reading for deaf-blind people

3. **Keyboard navigation:** Spacebar, arrow keys, letter shortcuts

4. **Proper labeling:** Clear, descriptive labels for all buttons

5. **State communications:** aria-pressed indicating toggle state

6. **Time announcements:** Progress updates available to screen readers

7. **User preferences:** Caption updates available to screen readers

This implementation ensures that screen readers can fully control and understand the media player's state and content.

CHAPTER 5   ACCESSIBLE VIDEOS AND AUDIO

Tools and Libraries for Captions

Creating accurate captions and transcripts can be time-consuming. But fortunately a huge ecosystem of tools exists to streamline this process.

Whenever you are generating caption files from scratch, editing autogenerated transcripts, or implementing accessible media players, using the right tools can reduce development time while ensuring compliance with accessibility standards.

AMARA stands out as a comprehensive web-based caption editor that supports collaborative editing, multiple subtitle formats, etc.

For desktop workflows, WGBH's CADET provides offline editing capabilities with advanced features like waveform visualization and keyboard shortcuts and also includes WebVTT and SRT.

Rather than implementing a web player yourself (which you can do because it's good practice), you can use the ABLE Player, available at `https://ableplayer.github.io/ableplayer/`.

It is an HTML accessible player.

In this section, we heavily focused on videos, so let's now focus on audio.

Accessible Audio Content

Audio-only content like podcasts, music, interviews, audio books, and sound recordings presents a challenge that differs from video.

Unlike video, for audio you need to add a transcription.

The primary accessibility barrier for audio content affects users who are deaf or have hard hearing.

Transcripts represent the cornerstone of audio accessibility. Unlike video captions that require precise timing and synchronization, audio transcripts can be more flexible in format while maintaining comprehensive content coverage.

Consider this transcript:

```
**Dr. Sarah Chen (Host):** Welcome to TechTalk Daily. I'm Dr.
Sarah Chen.
 **Marcus Rivera (Guest):** Thanks for having me, Sarah. I'm excited
to discuss our new accessibility framework.
 [Background music fades out]
 **Dr. Chen:** Let's start with the basics. What problem does this
framework solve?
```

[Phone notification sound]
Rivera: Sorry about that notification. The framework addresses...

Here is a simple implementation for the HTML audio player:

```
<audio controls preload="metadata" aria-labelledby="audio-title">
  <source src="podcast-episode.mp3" type="audio/mpeg">
  <source src="podcast-episode.ogg" type="audio/ogg">
  <p>Your browser doesn't support HTML5 audio.
     <a href="podcast-episode.mp3">Download the audio file</a>.</p>
</audio>
<h3 id="audio-title">Episode 15: Accessibility in Mobile Apps</h3>
```

You need to think on keyboard accessibility, screen reader compatibility, and playback speed and control.

When providing files, provide several formats like MP3 and OGG files. MP3 remains most universal supported format, but including the OGG format can improve compatibility with open-source browsers and assistive technologies.

Also think about progressive enhancement. Start with accessible HTML5 audio elements and enhance them with additional features rather than building entirely custom solutions that might bypass built-in accessibility features.

Here is an example with content:

```
<article class="audio-content">
  <header>
    <h2>Understanding ARIA Labels</h2>
    <p>Published: <time datetime="2025-06-14">June 14, 2025</time>
    </p>
    <p>Duration: 23 minutes</p>
    <p>Topics: Web development, Accessibility, ARIA</p>
  </header>

  <audio controls preload="metadata" aria-labelledby="audio-title">
    <source src="aria-labels-tutorial.mp3" type="audio/mpeg">
    <source src="aria-labels-tutorial.ogg" type="audio/ogg">
    <p>Your browser doesn't support HTML5 audio.
```

```
        <a href="aria-labels-tutorial.mp3">Download the audio
        file</a>.</p>
</audio>

<section class="transcript">
  <h3>Full Transcript</h3>
  <div class="transcript-content">
    <p><strong>Sarah (Host):</strong> Welcome to Web Dev Weekly.
    I'm Sarah, and today we're talking about ARIA labels with
    accessibility expert Mike Chen.</p>

    <p><strong>Mike:</strong> Thanks for having me, Sarah. ARIA
    labels are one of the most important tools for making web
    content accessible.</p>

    <p><strong>Sarah:</strong> Let's start with the basics. What
    exactly is an ARIA label?</p>

    <p><strong>Mike:</strong> ARIA stands for Accessible Rich
    Internet Applications. An ARIA label provides an accessible
    name for an element when the visual label isn't sufficient for
    screen readers.</p>

    <p><em>[Keyboard typing sounds]</em></p>

    <p><strong>Sarah:</strong> Can you give us a practical
    example?</p>

    <p><strong>Mike:</strong> Sure! Imagine a search button that
    only shows a magnifying glass icon. A screen reader user
    wouldn't know what that button does. But if we add aria-
    label="Search", now it's clear.</p>

    <p><strong>Sarah:</strong> That makes perfect sense. What's the
    difference between aria-label and aria-labelledby?</p>

    <p><strong>Mike:</strong> Great question. aria-label lets you
    write the label directly in the attribute. aria-labelledby
    references another element's text...</p>

    <p><em>[Content continues...]</em></p>
```

```
        </div>
      </section>
    </article>
```

Key features here include a semantic HTML structure, multiple audio formats, fallback download link, complete transcript, sound description, and clear content hierarchy.

This creates a fully accessible audio experience that works for all users.

But you might be asking, when should audio play? Should a screen reader read while the audio is playing?

Generally, no.

Screen readers should *not* automatically read while audio is playing. This should be chosen by the user.

The recommended behavior is that the audio plays normally while screen readers should *not* automatically read audio content while it's playing.

Audio plays normally while screen reader remain silent about audio content itself. This prevents the following:

- Audio conflicts (screen reader voice + original audio)
- Confusion for users who can hear original audio
- Unwanted interruptions for listening experience

```
<!-- This audio plays normally without screen reader interference -->
<audio controls>
    <source src="podcast.mp3" type="audio/mpeg">
  </audio>

  <!-- Transcript available separately -->
  <section class="transcript">
    <h3>Transcript</h3>
    <p>Users can access this transcript independently if needed</p>
  </section>
```

For deaf-blind users who need content via a braille display or speech, here is some example code:

```
    <div class="audio-player">
      <audio controls id="mainAudio">
```

```html
        <source src="interview.mp3" type="audio/mpeg">
    </audio>

    <!-- Optional: Live region for transcript announcements -->
    <div id="transcriptLive"
        class="sr-only"
        aria-live="polite"
        aria-atomic="false"></div>

    <!-- User preference toggle -->
    <label>
      <input type="checkbox" id="announceTranscript">
      Read transcript aloud while playing (for deaf-blind users)
    </label>
  </div>
```

```js
const audio = document.getElementById('mainAudio');
const transcriptLive = document.getElementById('transcriptLive');
const announceToggle = document.getElementById('announceTranscript');

// Only announce transcript if user specifically enables it
audio.addEventListener('timeupdate', () => {
  if (announceToggle.checked) {
    // Find current transcript text based on time
    const currentText = getCurrentTranscriptText(audio.currentTime);
    if (currentText) {
      transcriptLive.textContent = currentText;
    }
  }
});

function getCurrentTranscriptText(currentTime) {
  // Logic to find transcript text for current timestamp
  // This would match audio time to transcript portions
}
```

User choice is key here.

CHAPTER 5   ACCESSIBLE VIDEOS AND AUDIO

Creating accessible video and audio content isn't just about meeting compliance requirements; it's about building a digital experience that works for everyone.

Remember these principles:

- **Start with standards:** Use semantic HTML5 media elements as your foundation.

- **Provide alternatives:** Every audio elements needs text alternatives through transcripts or captions.

- **Test with real users:** Accessibility isn't complete without testing with actual assistive technologies.

- **Make it optional:** Give users control over accessibility features rather than forcing them.

- **Quality matters:** Accurate, well-formatted transcripts and captions are crucial for effective accessibility.

By following the techniques and examples covered in this book, you will create an accessible media that will contribute to an inclusive Web where everyone can participate fully in our increasingly connected digital world.

Summary and Next Steps

Here are the key takeaways from this chapter:

- **Captions and screen readers:** All videos must have text alternatives and also need to be synchronized.

- **Basic accessible media controls:** You learned how to implement basic media controls in videos.

- **Libraries that you can use:** There are some good tools for developers to use that make working with media easy.

You now have some nice tools in your toolkit. In the next chapter, you will learn how to create accessible forms.

89

CHAPTER 6

Accessible Forms

Forms are the gateways of the Web. Forms are how users register, log in, make purchases, contact customer support, and interact with countless online services. They are especially important when it comes to accessibility and, if not handled correctly, can create a barrier for millions of users.

When designing forms, you need to create forms that everyone can submit and fill. This includes the users who use keyboards to navigate instead of the mouse, people who rely on screen readers to understand page content, people with cognitive differences who benefit from clear instruction, and users with motor impairments who need larger click targets.

This is not only about creating a nice experience for users, but accessible forms are a requirement of WCAG and laws.

Forms need to have clear instructions, descriptive labels, correct colors, large enough text, and correct groupings. The form should communicate its name and role for each input state for assistive technologies like screen readers.

Also, as mentioned, keyboards are a big part of form accessibility. Every element in a form (button, input, etc.) needs to be interactive and reachable with the keyboard. This very much improves the usability for users with disabilities.

In this chapter, we will focus on HTML/CSS/JavaScript and the fundamentals of building accessible forms. We will start with semantic HTML that provides meaning to assistive technologies, then look at the CSS to enhance usability without sacrificing usability, and finally see how JavaScript can create helpful interactions.

Everything that you learn in this chapter is simply a good practice that should be common during your development.

CHAPTER 6   ACCESSIBLE FORMS

Semantic HTML

The most important part of semantic HTML when creating forms is to use native HTML controls like <input>, <select>, <button>, <textarea>, etc. They automatically communicate purpose, state, and behavior to the screen.

When the user encounters a <button>, for example, their screen reader immediately announces that it's a button that they can activate. As you are learning to build accessible forms, resist the temptation to reinvent the wheel. The native HTML elements should be used.

After using the semantic HTML elements, connect fields with descriptions. Every form field must have a clear, visible label that explains information to the user. Screen reader users rely on these labels to understand each field's purpose.

You can use the for attribute to connect a label to any input with a matching ID.

Connecting with Labels

The relationship between labels and form fields is the cornerstone of the accessible form design. Without proper labels, fields become mysterious black boxes that leave users, especially those with assistive technologies, guessing what information to provide.

Why do labels matter so much?

When a user with a screen reader navigates to an unlabeled input field, they might hear something generic like "text field" or "edit text." This provides no indication what belongs in that field. With a proper label, the user will hear the following:"Email address, edit text" "First name required, edit text".

Here's an example:

```
<label for="user-email">Email Address:</label>
<input id="user-email" name="email" type="email" />
```

Alternatively, you can wrap it like this:

```
<label>
    Email Address:
    <input name="email" type="email" />
</label>
```

When they are properly associated, screen readers announce both the label and the text as the user navigates to the control.

Also, you need to write descriptive label text.

The words you choose significantly impact usability. Simple names like "Name" or "Phone" force users to make assumptions about what specific information you want.

Instead, be precise and descriptive. For example:

- Instead of "Name," use "Full Name" or separate "First Name" and "Last Name."

- Instead of "Phone," use "Mobile Phone" and "Home Phone Number."

- Instead of "Address," use "Billing Address", "Shipping Address," etc.

But some forms fields require a little more complex handling strategy.

For form fields that need both primary and additional context, you can use aria-describedby.

```
<label for="account-number">Account Number:</label>
<input
  id="account-number"
  name="account"
  type="text"
  aria-describedby="account-help"
/>
<small id="account-help">
  Find this 10-digit number on your monthly statement
</small>
```

This approach ensures that the primary label is always announced, while additional context is provided when needed. Screen readers would typically announce: "Account number, edit text, Find this 10-digit number on your monthly statement."

For fields with multiple pieces of related information, you might need to combine several techniques.

```
<label for="password">
   New Password <span class="required">(required)</span>
</label>
<input
```

```
    id="password"
    type="password"
    required
    aria-describedby="password-requirements"
/>
<div id="password-requirements">
  Must be at least 8 characters with one number and one special
  character
</div>
```

Common Mistakes to Avoid When Labeling

One frequent error is to use placeholder text instead of the proper label.

Placeholders disappear when the user starts typing, leaving them without guidance if they need to review or correct their input. Placeholders are also not reliably announced by screen readers, making them bad for accessibility.

Another mistake is creating labels that are visual only. Sometimes designers create beautiful forms with labels that are conveyed through visual positioning or colors. Text positioned under the heading may be visually beautiful, but screen readers can't infer this relationship without proper HTML markup.

When using JavaScript to dynamically update the labels, make sure that they are announced to the screen readers using live regions when needed.

Make sure to test. If you do not own a screen reader, try with eyes closed with assistive software.

Ask yourself the following questions:

- Does each field announcement provide enough information to complete the form successfully?

- Can you understand the purpose of every field based on what you hear?

Grouping Related Fields Together

When forms contain multiple related questions or a set of questions, proper grouping is a must for user navigation. Without clear grouping, users, especially those with assistive technologies, may struggle to understand which fields belong together.

Consider a form asking users for their email, phone, and mailing address. Without proper grouping, the user may encounter following: "Email radio button" followed by "Phone radio button" without understanding that they are mutually exclusive options answering the same question.

The HTML <fieldset> and <legend> elements provide the primary mechanism for creating meaningful field groups. The fieldset creates a semantic boundary around related form controls, while the legend serves as the group's accessible title.

Here's an example:

```
<fieldset>
    <legend>How would you prefer to receive updates?</legend>
    <label>
      <input type="radio" name="contact-preference" value="email" />
      Email notifications
    </label>
    <label>
      <input type="radio" name="contact-preference" value="sms" />
      Text messages
    </label>
    <label>
      <input type="radio" name="contact-preference" value="mail" />
      Postal mail
    </label>
    <label>
      <input type="radio" name="contact-preference" value="none" />
      No updates
    </label>
</fieldset>
```

When the screen reader navigates to this fieldset, it will hear "How would you prefer to receive updates?"

Without this grouping, users will encounter each option in isolation, which can cause confusion.

Check boxes also benefit from fieldset grouping, as shown here:

```
<fieldset>
    <legend>Which programming languages do you use regularly?</legend>
    <label>
      <input type="checkbox" name="languages" value="javascript" />
      JavaScript
    </label>
    <label>
      <input type="checkbox" name="languages" value="python" />
      Python
    </label>
    <label>
      <input type="checkbox" name="languages" value="java" />
      Java
    </label>
    <label>
      <input type="checkbox" name="languages" value="csharp" />
      C#
    </label>
</Fieldset>
```

Common Mistakes to Avoid When Grouping

One frequent error is overusing fieldsets, wrapping every individual form field in its own set.

This hinders navigation. Use fieldsets only when you have genually related fields that benefit from being grouped.

Another mistake is creating groupings that are too large.

A field set that contains everything from name to favorite color can lead to confusion. Keep them focused and logical.

Failing to provide legends for fieldsets is equally problematic. A fieldset without a legend provides no context about why the fields are grouped together, hiding the purpose of grouping altogether.

Keyboard Navigation

Keyboard navigation is a fundamental aspect of web accessibility.

Many users rely entirely on keyboard navigation, whether due motor disabilities, visual impairments, or simply preference.

Understanding how tab order and tabIndex work is crucial.

Before diving into tabIndex, it's essential to understand that HTML elements have a natural keyboard navigation based on position in document.

When you press the Tab key, focus moves through the elements, links, buttons, form inputs, etc., in the order that they appear in the HTML source code.

This works when it's simple and logical.

Consider this simple form:

```
<form>
  <label for="name">Full Name:</label>
  <input id="name" type="text" />

  <label for="email">Email:</label>
  <input id="email" type="email" />

  <label for="message">Message:</label>
  <textarea id="message"></textarea>

  <button type="submit">Send Message</button>
</form>
```

The user can use Tab to go through this form in a logical sequence.

But what happens when tab order goes wrong?

The tabindex attribute controls whether something can receive the keyboard focus and influences the order that elements are navigated in.

- tabindex="0" makes an element focusable and includes it in natural tab order.
- tabindex="-1" makes an element focusable programmatically but removes it from the natural order.

A positive number creates a custom tab order.

CHAPTER 6 ACCESSIBLE FORMS

While positive numbers in tabindex seem like an easy solution for controlling tab order, they create more problems than they solve. Elements with positive tab numbers are always focused on before elements with a tab index of 0 or no tab index attribute, regardless of their position in the HTML.

This creates confusing navigation patterns:

```
<!-- Don't do this -->
<input type="text" tabindex="2" placeholder="This field comes second" />
<input type="text" tabindex="1" placeholder="But this one is focused first" />
<input type="text" placeholder="And this one comes last, even though it's visually in the middle" />
```

If you are working on a team of developers and you add a positive number, the navigation becomes unpredictable and difficult to maintain. It is far better to structure your HTML in the correct order from the start.

Correct Usage of Tab Index in Forms

Sometimes you need to make an element focusable that is not interactive by default. Custom form controls or error message might need to receive focus programmatically, as shown here:

```
<div id="error-message" tabindex="-1" role="alert">
    Please correct the following errors before submitting:
</div>
```

The tabindex -1 allow you to focus this error message with JavaScript when navigation fails, but it won't mess with the normal tab navigation.

In forms that are dynamic, appearing dynamically, you need to add a programmatic tab index, as shown here:

```
<fieldset>
    <legend>Do you have a company?</legend>
    <label>
      <input type="radio" name="hasCompany" value="yes" />
      Yes
    </label>
```

```html
      <label>
        <input type="radio" name="hasCompany" value="no" />
        No
      </label>
    </fieldset>

    <div id="company-section" class="company-fields hidden">
      <label for="company-name">Company Name:</label>
      <input id="company-name" type="text" tabindex="-1" />
    </div>
```

```css
.company-fields.hidden {
    display: none;
  }

  .company-fields.visible {
    display: block;
  }
```

```javascript
// Wait for the DOM to be fully loaded
document.addEventListener('DOMContentLoaded', function() {
    const companyRadios = document.querySelectorAll('input[name="hasCo
    mpany"]');
    const companySection = document.getElementById('company-section');
    const companyNameField = document.getElementById('company-name');

    // Add event listeners to both radio buttons
    companyRadios.forEach(function(radio) {
      radio.addEventListener('change', function() {
        if (this.value === 'yes') {
          showCompanyFields();
        } else {
          hideCompanyFields();
        }
      });
    });

    function showCompanyFields() {
      companySection.classList.remove('hidden');
```

```
    companySection.classList.add('visible');
    companyNameField.tabIndex = 0; // Make it part of tab order
    companyNameField.focus(); // Draw attention to the new field
  }
  function hideCompanyFields() {
    companySection.classList.add('hidden');
    companySection.classList.remove('visible');
    companyNameField.tabIndex = -1; // Remove from tab order
  }
});
```

Testing the Keyboard Navigation

The most effective way to test keyboard navigation is to use it yourself. For example, try completing your entire form using only the Tab key, Shift+Tab (to go backward), Enter, and the spacebar.

Pay attention to the following:

- Does the focus move in logical order that matches visual layout?
- Can you reach every interactive element?
- Is it always clear which element has the focus?
- Are any elements that trap focus?
- Can you complete all the interaction on the form without a mouse?

Of course, test with screen readers. Screen readers often navigate by jumping between form fields, so the logical tab becomes even more critical.

Tab Order and Screen Readers

Screen reader users often usually navigate through the forms by jumping between fields and using special keyboard shortcuts rather than pressing Tab to go through elements.

However, the tab order is still very important.

When using "next form field" commands, screen readers typically follow the same order as tab navigation. If the user goes through the form, they will encounter the same sequence as other keyboard users.

Common Mistakes to Avoid

Avoid the following:

- **Ignoring logical flow:** Using CSS to create complex layouts without considering keyboard navigation order leads to a confusing experience. You need to always test the tab order.

- **Custom controls that are not accessible:** When creating custom form controls like styled drop-downs or toggle switches, developers sometimes forget to make them keyboard accessible. Ensure that all custom controls can be focused on via the keyboard.

Some developers remove focus indicators entirely for aesthetic reasons. This makes it impossible to see where the users are inside the form. Always provide the focus indicators.

Accessible Forms and Error Handling

Error handling is very important.

It's often where form accessibility succeeds or fails. When validation messages are not clear, poorly positioned, or invisible to assistive technologies, they can really degrade the user experience.

Accessible error handling is more than providing red text. The errors need to be understandable. Users need to know that an error happened, understand what went wrong, and know how to correct the problem.

The most fundamental requirement is ensuring error messages are programmatically associated with their form fields.

Without this connection, screen readers users may hear some error that is on the page but struggle to find where it is coming from.

When a validation error occurs, screen reader users need immediate notification. ARIA live regions are very helpful for this.

```
<div id="error-announcer" aria-live="polite" aria-atomic="true" class="sr-only">
    <!-- Error announcements will be inserted here -->
</div>
```

```
<label for="email-field">Email Address:</label>
<input
  id="email-field"
  type="email"
  aria-describedby="email-error"
  aria-invalid="false"
/>
<div id="email-error" class="error-message" style="display: none;"></div
```

The aria-live="polite" attribute ensures that error messages are announced when the user finishes their current action, while aria-atomic="true" means that the entire message content is read each time it changes.

The sr-only class visually hides the announcer while keeping it available to the screen reader.

When an error occurs, you can update both the visible error message and the live region. Here's an example:

```
function showEmailError(message) {
  const emailField = document.getElementById('email-field');
  const errorDiv = document.getElementById('email-error');
  const announcer = document.getElementById('error-announcer');

  // Update field state
  emailField.setAttribute('aria-invalid', 'true');

  // Show visible error message
  errorDiv.textContent = message;
  errorDiv.style.display = 'block';

  // Announce to screen readers
  announcer.textContent = `Email field: ${message}`;
}
```

Error messages must be positioned where the user can find them easily and must be connected to their fields. The most reliable approach places error messages immediately after their associated field using aria-describedby to create the connection.

```
<label for="password">Password:</label>
<input
  id="password"
  type="password"
  aria-describedby="password-requirements password-error"
  aria-invalid="false"
  required
/>
<div id="password-requirements">
  Must be at least 8 characters with one number and one special character
</div>
<div id="password-error" class="error-message" style="display: none;"></div>
```

You also need to create understandable messages.

Poor error messages:

- "Invalid email"
- "Wrong format"
- "Field required"

Better error messages:

- "Please enter a valid email address like name@example.com"
- "Phone number should be in format (555) 123-4567"
- "First name is required to create your account"

Also, do not neglect design considerations when it comes to errors. An error should be noticeable without relying solely on color so that users who are color blind do not miss any text.

```
.error-message {
  color: #d32f2f;
  font-weight: 500;
  display: flex;
  align-items: flex-start;
```

```css
    gap: 0.5rem;
    margin-top: 0.25rem;
}

.error-message::before {
    content: "⚠";
    color: #d32f2f;
    font-weight: bold;
    flex-shrink: 0;
}

.field-error {
    border: 2px solid #d32f2f;
    background-color: #ffeaea;
}

.field-error:focus {
    outline: 3px solid #d32f2f;
    outline-offset: 2px;
}
```

This approach use colors, icons, border changes, and background colors to ensure errors are seen.

Also keep accessibility in mind when designing success states.

When users submit forms, correct errors, etc., provide clear information.

Here is how to test if your form is accessible:

1. **Keyboard navigation:** Try completing the form with errors using only the keyboard. Can you identify and reach error messages easily?

2. **Screen reader testing:** Use a screen reader to see if the error-to-field relationship is clear.

3. **Have someone unfamiliar with form try to correct errors:** Can they do it easily?

Summary and Next Steps

As you know, forms are the gateway of the Web! Here are the key takeaways from this chapter:

- **Building forms starts with semantic HTML:** You need to start building forms with semantic HTML.

- **Connecting with labels:** Labels are needed for the form fields.

- **Grouping related elements together:** Grouping together common fields is a must.

- **Ensuring keyboard navigation and error handling are accessible:** You must enable users to use keyboard to navigate forms and also properly handle errors. Error handling is a place where accessible forms fail or succeed. Pay extra attention here. It's more than putting a red border around input.

The next chapter explains how to use the most popular frameworks and libraries to create an accessible experience.

CHAPTER 7

SPAs and Modern Front-End Frameworks and Accessibility

As you are aware, web accessibility ensures that websites and web applications are usable by everyone. As a developer, when you use a framework or library such as React, Vue, or Angular, you have a responsibility to create applications for users regardless of their abilities or browsing preferences.

Modern frameworks have transformed how you build web applications, as well as have introduced many accessibility challenges. Single-page applications (SPAs), dynamic content updates, and a complex component hierarchy can introduce barriers for screen readers and other assistive technologies. The good news that each of these frameworks provides tools to help developers create accessible applications.

For example, having a complex hierarchy of components, one of the biggest features of modern frameworks, can break a basic semantic HTML structure.

A button component can render perfectly visually but lose its connection to the form label when it is part of a parent component, creating confusion for screen readers.

The Virtual DOM, while enabling good performance updates, can also disrupt assistive technologies that rely on a DOM reference. Components re-render with frameworks. When a component re-renders, screen readers might lose their place in complex user interfaces, forcing users to start again.

In addition, heavy use of <div> elements rather than semantic HTML can cause problems.

In this chapter, you will explore accessibility principles in React, Vue, and Angular and dive deep into best practices when using them.

Whether you are working with React, Vue, or Angular, the core principles remain the same. You are building for all users, which means that everyone can use what you create.

Each framework has own unique characteristics when it comes to accessibility, but keep in mind that everything you have learned in previous chapters is still valid.

We will focus on screen readers, keyboard navigation, ARIA, and tools and testing. This chapter assumes that you know the basics of how to use these frameworks.

React

Let's start with React, a UI library that ultimately renders standard HTML in a browser.

Screen Readers and Basic Markup and Components

Largely, accessibility in React means using right HTML elements. But you must use them correctly in JSX.

JSX makes it straightforward to write semantic HTML. It is easy to fall into the trap called div soup, but you need to use semantic elements, because, as you learned, screen readers rely on semantic elements.

Here's an example:

```
// Poor screen reader support
function Navigation() {
  return (
    <div className="nav">
      <div className="nav-item" onClick={handleHome}>Home</div>
      <div className="nav-item" onClick={handleAbout}>About</div>
    </div>
  );
}

// Excellent screen reader support
function Navigation() {
  return (
    <nav aria-label="Main navigation">
```

```
      <ul>
        <li><button onClick={handleHome}>Home</button></li>
        <li><button onClick={handleAbout}>About</button></li>
      </ul>
    </nav>
  );
}
```

The semantic version provides multiple benefits: the <nav> element creates a landmark region that the screen can jump to directly. The list also has a relationship to the elements.

A button element automatically conveys its interactive nature. When you replace it with <div> and add an onClick handler, you lose the built-in functionality and must manually re-create it with ARIA.

Here's another example:

```
function ActionButton({ onClick, children }) {
  return (
    <div className="button-style" onClick={onClick}>
      {children}
    </div>
  );
}
```

These are the issues:

- **No semantic meaning:** It uses a generic <div> instead of a proper <button> element.

- **Missing keyboard support:** <div> elements are not focusable by default and do not respond to the Enter key or spacebar.

- **Poor accessibility:** Screen readers will not recognize this as an interactive button.

- **Requires extra CSS:** It needs extra CSS code for the cursor, colors, etc.

Here is a better example:

```
function ActionButton({ onClick, children }) {
  return (
    <button type="button" onClick={onClick}>
      {children}
    </button>
  );
}
```

These are the improvements:

- **Semantic HTML:** It uses the proper <button> element.
- **Keyboard support:** It automatically responds to Enter/spacebar.
- **Screen readers:** Screen readers understand that it's a clickable button.
- **No need for CSS:** There is no extra browser styling needed.

Here is an example of the best implementation:

```
function ActionButton({
  onClick,
  children,
  ariaLabel,
  disabled = false,
  type = "button"
}) {
  return (
    <button
      type={type}
      onClick={onClick}
      aria-label={ariaLabel}
      disabled={disabled}
    >
      {children}
    </button>
  );
}
```

Why is this one the best?

- **Enhanced accessibility:** The aria-label provides additional context for screen readers, which is especially useful when the button might be the only icon.

- **disabled:** There is a properly disabled button, and the code communicates this state to assistive technologies.

- **type:** This code allows you to specify "button", "submit", or "reset" depending on the context.

Here is another example:

```
<ActionButton onClick={handleSave}>Save</ActionButton>
```

As you can see, you can have default values inside components. With more advanced usage, you can do the following:

```
<ActionButton
  onClick={handleDelete}
  ariaLabel="Delete user account permanently"
  disabled={isLoading}
  type="button"
>
  🗑
</ActionButton>
```

These examples show how to build increasingly robust, accessible components that work well for all users, including those who use assistive technologies.

Let's look at another example that is more complex:

```
function BlogPost({ post }) {
  return (
    <div className="blog-post">
      <div className="title">{post.title}</div>
      <div className="meta">By {post.author} on {post.date}</div>
      <div className="content">{post.content}</div>
      <div className="sidebar">
        <div className="related-title">Related Posts</div>
```

```
          <div className="related-posts">
            {post.related.map(item => (
              <div key={item.id} className="related-item">
                {item.title}
              </div>
            ))}
          </div>
        </div>
      </div>
    );
  }
```

These are the problems with the previous code:

- **Div soup:** Everything appears as generic <div> elements/containers.

- **No document outline:** Assistive technologies will have trouble building meaningful page structure.

- **Keyboard accessibility:** It is not keyboard accessible; it has no click indications.

Here is the next example:

```
function BlogPost({ post }) {
  return (
    <article>
      <header>
        <h1>{post.title}</h1>
        <div className="post-meta">
          <span>By <strong>{post.author}</strong></span>
          <time dateTime={post.isoDate}>{post.date}</time>
        </div>
      </header>

      <div className="post-content">
        {post.content}
      </div>
```

```
    <aside aria-labelledby="related-heading">
      <h2 id="related-heading">Related Posts</h2>
      <nav aria-label="Related posts">
        <ul>
          {post.related.map(item => (
            <li key={item.id}>
              <a href={item.url}>{item.title}</a>
            </li>
          ))}
        </ul>
      </nav>
    </aside>
  </article>
  );
}
```

Here is what is happening in this example:

- **<article>** tells the screen reader that it is stand-alone content.
- **<header>** clearly marks the introductory information.
- **<h1>** establishes the proper hierarchy for navigation.

  Here is the real-world impact:

  - **First version:** "Blog post, title, meta, content, sidebar..." (very confusing)
  - **Second version:** "Article, heading level 1, etc." (clear structure)

  Keyboard navigation:

  - **First version:** The Tab key may skip completely noninteractive <div> elements.
  - **Second version:** There is a logical tab order.

Accessibility standards have been met.

useState and Accessibility

Let's look at an example of useState. Specifically, let's create an expandable section component.

This component demonstrates several semantic principles: the section element provides a nice document structure, the h3 provides proper heading hierarchy, the button clearly shows that it's interactive, aria-expanded communicates the current state, ARIA controls establish a relationship between the trigger the and content, and aria-hidden shows it all to screen readers.

The result is that the interface works for the keyboard, the mouse, and assistive technologies.

This example uses the React hook: useState.

```
function ExpandableSection({ title, children, defaultExpanded = false }) {
   const [isExpanded, setIsExpanded] = useState(defaultExpanded);
   const contentId = useId();

   return (
     <section>
       <h3>
         <button
           type="button"
           aria-expanded={isExpanded}
           aria-controls={contentId}
           onClick={() => setIsExpanded(!isExpanded)}
           className="expand-button"
         >
           {title}
           <span aria-hidden="true" className="expand-icon">
             {isExpanded ? '−' : '+'}
           </span>
         </button>
       </h3>
```

```
      <div
        id={contentId}
        className={`expandable-content ${isExpanded ? 'expanded' :
        'collapsed'}`}
        aria-hidden={!isExpanded}
      >
        {children}
      </div>
    </section>
  );
}
```

```
const [isExpanded, setIsExpanded] = useState(defaultExpanded);
```

The React useState hook allows components to manage state. (You can learn more about the useState hook at https://react.dev/reference/react/hooks.)

Here it tracks whether the section is expanded or collapsed.

```
const contentId = useId();
```

Here useId generates unique, stable IDs. This prevents ID collision when multiple ExpandableSection components exist on the same page.

Here are the accessibility features:

- A proper semantic structure

  ```
  <section>
          <h3>
              <button
  ```

- ARIA states and properties

  ```
  aria-expanded={isExpanded}
  aria-controls={contentId}
  ```

  Why does this matter?

  - aria-expanded: Tells screen readers whether a section is currently opened or closed
  - aria-controls: Creates a programmatic relationship between a button and the content it controls

Screen readers will announce "Button, expanded" or "Button, collapsed."

```
// Safe to use multiple times the component
<ExpandableSection title="FAQ 1">...</ExpandableSection>
<ExpandableSection title="FAQ 2">...</ExpandableSection>
```

The component adheres to the WCAG guidelines.

This component demonstrates how combining React built-in hooks with proper semantic HTML and ARIA attributes creates truly accessible elements that work for everyone.

useEffect and Accessibility

The following LiveRegionAnnouncer component is an excellent example of using useEffect for accessibility side effects. I will show you the code and then break down why it's important. (You can learn more about useEffect at https://react.dev/reference/react/useEffect.)

As you learned, a live region is an ARIA accessibility feature that announces dynamic content changes to screen readers, without requiring user interaction or a focus change.

Let's break down the component:

```
function LiveRegionAnnouncer() {
  const [announcement, setAnnouncement] = useState('');
  const [priority, setPriority] = useState('polite');
  const timeoutRef = useRef(null);

  // Clear announcements after they've been read
  useEffect(() => {
    if (announcement) {
      // Clear any existing timeout
      if (timeoutRef.current) {
        clearTimeout(timeoutRef.current);
      }

      // Clear the announcement after a brief delay to allow re-announcements
```

```
      timeoutRef.current = setTimeout(() => {
        setAnnouncement('');
      }, 1000);
    }

    return () => {
      if (timeoutRef.current) {
        clearTimeout(timeoutRef.current);
      }
    };
  }, [announcement]);

  const announce = (message, urgency = 'polite') => {
    setPriority(urgency);
    setAnnouncement(message);
  };

  return (
      <div
        aria-live={priority}
        aria-atomic="true"
        className="sr-only"
      >
        {announcement}
      </div>
      {/* Component that uses announce function */}
    );
}
```

Here is an example of state management:

```
const [announcement, setAnnouncement] = useState('');
const [priority, setPriority] = useState('polite');
const timeoutRef = useRef(null);
```

- **announcement:** Stores the message to be announced
- **priority:** Controls the urgency ('polite') or ('assertive')
- **timeoutRef:** Manages cleanup timing

As mentioned in the React documentation, the useEffect hook is a React hook that synchronizes a component with the external system.

You may be wondering what is the external system here. The external system is screen reader technology.

```
useEffect(() => {
  if (announcement) {
    // Clear any existing timeout
    if (timeoutRef.current) {
      clearTimeout(timeoutRef.current);
    }

    // Clear the announcement after a brief delay
    timeoutRef.current = setTimeout(() => {
      setAnnouncement('');
    }, 1000);
  }
  return () => {
    if (timeoutRef.current) {
      clearTimeout(timeoutRef.current);
    }
  };
}, [announcement]);
```

Why is the useEffect pattern critical here?

- **Side effect management**

    useEffect allows you to perform side effects.

    Here are the side effects:
    - Setting the timeouts for announcement cleanup
    - Managing the lifecycle of the screen reader announcement

- **Dependency array [announcement]:**

  When you specify dependencies, our effects run after initial render and after re-renders with changed dependencies. The effect runs only when announcement is changed.

  This ensures:

  – New announcements trigger the cleanup/reset cycle

  – Unchanged announcements do not cause re-runs

The cleanup function prevents memory leaks from abandoned timeouts, etc.

```
<div
  aria-live={priority}
  aria-atomic="true"
  className="sr-only"
>
  {announcement}
</div>
```

Here you use ARIA attributes:

aria-live={priority}: **'polite'** waits for speech to finish, **'assertive'** interrupts immediately.

aria-atomic="true": Screen readers announce the entire content, not just changes.

className="sr-only": This makes the class visually hidden but available to screen readers.

Timeouts are very essential here:

```
timeoutRef.current = setTimeout(() => {
  setAnnouncement('');
}, 1000);
```

Without timeouts, you would have following problem:

Problem: If you set an announcement two times, screen readers will not announce it again because the content has not changed.

Solution: Clear the announcement after one second, allowing the same message multiple times.

Here is an example:

```
function FormSubmission() {
  const announce = useAnnouncer(); // Custom hook using
  LiveRegionAnnouncer

  const handleSubmit = async (data) => {
    try {
      await submitForm(data);
      announce("Form submitted successfully!", "polite");
    } catch (error) {
      announce("Error: Form submission failed!", "assertive");
    }
  };
}
```

The following are the real-world benefits:

- **Status updates:** "Loading Complete," "Item added to a cart"

- **Error notifications:** "Password must be 8 characters"

- **Success confirmations:** "Settings saved"

I wanted to demonstrate with the useEffects component when you need to "step outside of React" and synchronize with external systems. Screen reader APIs are exactly this type of external system; they exist outside the React rendering cycle but need to be synchronized with component state changes.

This pattern demonstrates how useEffect enables seamless interaction between React and accessibility APIs.

Testing and Linting

Creating accessible React applications requires testing and automated checks to catch accessibility issues before they reach users.

ESLINT Plugin JSX A11y

The JSX A11y plugin (https://www.npmjs.com/package/eslint-plugin-jsx-a11y) is essential for catching accessibility issues during development. This plugin analyzes JSX and warns about common accessibility violations, acting as a first line of defense for accessibility.

The plugin checks more than 30 rules in different accessibility categories.

```
  // ✗ This will trigger jsx-a11y/alt-text
<img src="profile.jpg" />
// ✓ Fixed version
<img src="profile.jpg" alt="User profile photo" />
// ✗ This will trigger jsx-a11y/aria-props (invalid ARIA attribute)
<div aria-labell="Navigation menu" />
// ✓ Fixed version
<div aria-label="Navigation menu" />
// ✗ This will trigger jsx-a11y/role-has-required-aria-props
<div role="button" />
// ✓ Fixed version with proper keyboard handling
<div
  role="button"
  tabIndex={0}
  onKeyDown={handleKeyDown}
  onClick={handleClick}
/>
```

Here is an example for interactive elements:

```
// ✗ This will trigger jsx-a11y/click-events-have-key-events
<div onClick={handleClick}>Click me</div>

// ✓ Fixed version
<div
  role="button"
  tabIndex={0}
  onClick={handleClick}
```

```
  onKeyDown={(e) => {
    if (e.key === 'Enter' || e.key === ' ') {
      handleClick();
    }
  }}
>
  Click me
</div>

// 🎯 Even better - use semantic HTML
<button onClick={handleClick}>Click me</button>
```

This is a basic checklist for screen readers:

- **Navigation:** Can the user navigate by headings, landmarks, and links?
- **Forms:** Are labels, errors, and text announced correctly?
- **Dynamic content:** Do live regions announce changes appropriately?
- **Focus management:** Does the focus move logically, and is it visible?
- **Interactive elements:** Are buttons, links, etc., clearly identified?

Vue

Vue.js (https://vuejs.org/) offers a unique approach to building accessible applications through its reactive templating system, single-file components, and progressive enhancement philosophy.

Unlike other frameworks, Vue declarative syntax makes it natural to write semantic HTML while maintaining the behavior of modern web applications.

The Vue reactivity system automatically updates ARIA attributes and announcements when the data changes. Popular components libraries for Vue (like Vuetify, Quasar, and PrimeVue) include built-in accessibility features.

The Vue Composition API provides powerful patterns for encapsulating accessibility logic into reusable components.

Let's explore how to use Vue for accessibility.

Screen Readers and Vue

The Vue template syntax encourages semantic HTML by making it easy to write accessible markup. The framework's single-file structure keeps template, styles, and logic organized, making accessibility even easier.

```
<!-- Poor screen reader support -->
<template>
    <div class="nav">
      <div class="nav-item" @click="goHome">Home</div>
      <div class="nav-item" @click="goAbout">About</div>
      <div class="nav-item" @click="goContact">Contact</div>
    </div>
  </template>

  <!-- Excellent screen reader support -->
  <template>
    <nav aria-label="Main navigation">
      <ul>
        <li><button @click="goHome" type="button">Home</button></li>
        <li><button @click="goAbout" type="button">About</button></li>
        <li><button @click="goContact" type="button">Contact</button></li>
      </ul>
    </nav>
  </template>
```

The semantic version creates the proper navigation landmark and makes it easy for users to navigate.

As mentioned, the Vue reactivity system shines when managing dynamic ARIA attributes, unlike frameworks that require manual DOM manipulation. Vue templates can bind ARIA directly to component data, ensuring screen readers always receive the current state information.

Vue-Accessible Accordion

The Vue accordion component demonstrates some nice accessibility practices:

```
<template>
    <div class="accordion">
      <h2>
        <button
          :aria-expanded="isExpanded"
          :aria-controls="contentId"
          @click="toggleExpanded"
          class="accordion-header"
        >
          {{ title }}
          <span aria-hidden="true" class="accordion-icon">
            {{ isExpanded ? '−' : '+' }}
          </span>
        </button>
      </h2>

      <div
        :id="contentId"
        :aria-hidden="!isExpanded"
        class="accordion-content"
        :class="{ 'expanded': isExpanded }"
      >
        <slot />
      </div>
    </div>
</template>

<script>
import { ref, computed } from 'vue'

export default {
  name: 'AccessibleAccordion',
  props: {
    title: {
```

```
      type: String,
      required: true
    },
    defaultExpanded: {
      type: Boolean,
      default: false
    }
  },
  setup(props) {
    const isExpanded = ref(props.defaultExpanded)
    const contentId = ref(`accordion-content-${Math.random().
    toString(36).substr(2, 9)}`)

    const toggleExpanded = () => {
      isExpanded.value = !isExpanded.value
    }

    return {
      isExpanded,
      contentId,
      toggleExpanded
    }
  }
}
</script>

    const isExpanded = ref(props.defaultExpanded)
    const contentId = ref(`accordion-content-${Math.random().
    toString(36).substr(2, 9)}`)
```

Let's break it down:

- **ref()** creates a reactive state that automatically updates the DOM when there are changes.

- **contentId** generates unique IDs to prevent conflicts when multiple accordions exist.

- **defaultExpanded** prop allows for flexible initial state.

This is a reactive method:

```
const toggleExpanded = () => {
  isExpanded.value = !isExpanded.value
}
```

Also, by looking at the HTML, you can see that it's semantic.

Having buttons inside headings is recommended by WCAG for implementing expandable sections. Screen readers use headings to find accordions quickly.

```
:aria-expanded="isExpanded"
:aria-controls="contentId"
```

Notice the two dots at the beginning of the previous code?

This is Vue's binding system, which updates this attribute reactively and announces to the screen readers "Button expanded" or "Button collapsed."

:aria-controls creates a programmatic relationship between the button and the content.

What are the advantages of Vue over vanilla JavaScript regarding accessibility?

– **Automatic updates:** There are no manual DOM updates required.

– **Single source of the truth:** isExpanded controls both ARIA and CSS states.

– **No sync issues:** Vue ensures ARIA attributes always match the component state.

Here is a real-world example:

```
<AccessibleAccordion title="Shipping Info" :default-expanded="true">
   <p>Free shipping on orders over $50</p>
 </AccessibleAccordion>

 <AccessibleAccordion title="Return Policy">
   <p>30-day return window</p>
 </AccessibleAccordion>
```

Let's look at the screen reader experience.

Navigation:

1. "Heading level 2, Shipping Info"
2. "Button expanded, shipping info"
3. Tab = Content is announced
4. Next heading = "Heading level 2, Return Policy"

Interaction:

- **Enter/Space** on button toggle
- **State changes** announced automatically
- **Hidden content** does not interfere with navigation

This component shows how a modern framework with reactivity can create an accessible experience. The declarative binding syntax makes ARIA impossible to forget or get out of sync, while Vue reactivity ensures screen readers receive accurate information.

The SPA Challenge

SPAs face a big problem with routes and changes.

Traditional multipage websites automatically announce page changes to screen readers, move focus to the top of the pages, and update the browser document title.

SPAs break this behavior because navigation happens via JavaScript without full-page reloads, leaving screen reader users unaware that the page has been changed.

Here is a simple Vue app called App.vue that demonstrates the accessibility route changing:

```
<template>
  <div id="app">
    <!-- Skip link -->
    <a href="#main-content" class="skip-link" @click="focusMain">
      Skip to main content
    </a>
```

```
    <!-- Live region for announcements -->
    <div aria-live="polite" class="sr-only" v-if="announcement">
      {{ announcement }}
    </div>

    <!-- Navigation -->
    <nav aria-label="Main navigation">
      <ul class="nav-list">
        <li><router-link to="/">Home</router-link></li>
        <li><router-link to="/about">About</router-link></li>
        <li><router-link to="/contact">Contact</router-link></li>
      </ul>
    </nav>

    <!-- Main content -->
    <main id="main-content" ref="mainContent" tabindex="-1">
      <router-view />
    </main>
  </div>
</template>

<script>
export default {
  name: 'App',
  data() {
    return {
      announcement: ''
    }
  },
  methods: {
    focusMain(event) {
      event.preventDefault()
      this.$refs.mainContent.focus()
      this.$refs.mainContent.scrollIntoView({ behavior: 'smooth' })
    },
```

```
    announcePageChange(pageName) {
      this.announcement = `Navigated to ${pageName} page`
      // Clear announcement after 1 second
      setTimeout(() => {
        this.announcement = ''
      }, 1000)
    }
  },
  watch: {
    $route(to, from) {
      // Announce page changes
      const pageName = to.meta?.title || to.name || 'new page'
      this.announcePageChange(pageName)

      // Focus main content
      setTimeout(() => {
        this.$refs.mainContent.focus()
      }, 100)
    }
  }
}
</script>
```

Here is the Router.js file:

```
import { createRouter, createWebHistory } from 'vue-router'
import Home from '../views/Home.vue'
import About from '../views/About.vue'
import Contact from '../views/Contact.vue'

const routes = [
  {
    path: '/',
    name: 'Home',
    component: Home,
```

```
    meta: {
      title: 'Home'
    }
  },
  {
    path: '/about',
    name: 'About',
    component: About,
    meta: {
      title: 'About Us'
    }
  },
  {
    path: '/contact',
    name: 'Contact',
    component: Contact,
    meta: {
      title: 'Contact'
    }
  }
]
const router = createRouter({
  history: createWebHistory(),
  routes
})
// Update page title for each route
router.afterEach((to) => {
  document.title = to.meta?.title
    ? `${to.meta.title} - My Website`
    : 'My Website'
})
export default router
```

Screen readers hear "Navigated to About Us Page" when routing changes and you use ARIA's live polite feature.

Here is how to test this:

1. **Keyboard only:** Use Tab, Enter, and the spacebar to navigate.
2. **Screen reader:** Test with NVDA (free) or VoiceOver (Mac).
3. **Focus visible:** Make sure you can see where the focus is.
4. **Route changes:** Listen for announcements when navigating.

This simple example shows how to make the Vue router accessible with just a few key techniques.

Testing and Linting

Like React, Vue has linting packages that are ready to use.

ESLINT Plugin: vuejs-accessibility

The vuejs-accessibility package (https://www.npmjs.com/package/eslint-plugin-vuejs-accessibility) is specially designed for Vue.js applications, providing automated accessibility checks that understand Vue template syntax, directives, and component patterns. This plugin recognizes Vue-specific patterns and can check Vue-accessibility issues unique to the Vue reactivity system.

```
<!-- ✗ This will trigger vuejs-accessibility/aria-props -->
<template>
   <div :aria-labell="buttonLabel">
     {{ buttonText }}
   </div>
</template>

<!-- ✓ Fixed version with correct ARIA attribute -->
<template>
   <div :aria-label="buttonLabel">
     {{ buttonText }}
   </div>
</template>
```

```
<!-- ✗ This will trigger vuejs-accessibility/click-events-have-key-events -->
<template>
    <div @click="handleClick">
      Click me
    </div>
</template>
```

Angular

The Angular approach to accessibility is both comprehensive and systematic. (Learn more at `https://angular.dev/overview`.)

The framework has an enterprise-focused philosophy of providing a robust, scalable solution out of the box. The amazing people who are working and building Angular have invested heavily into the accessibility infrastructure, most notable through Angular Component Development (CDK), which provides a collection of accessible features. The Angular CDK, known also as @angular/cdk/a11y, is one of the most mature libraries in the front-end ecosystem.

It provides solutions to focus management, screen reader support, keyboard navigation, and live announcements that are well tested in enterprise applications.

Figure 7-1 shows the file structure:

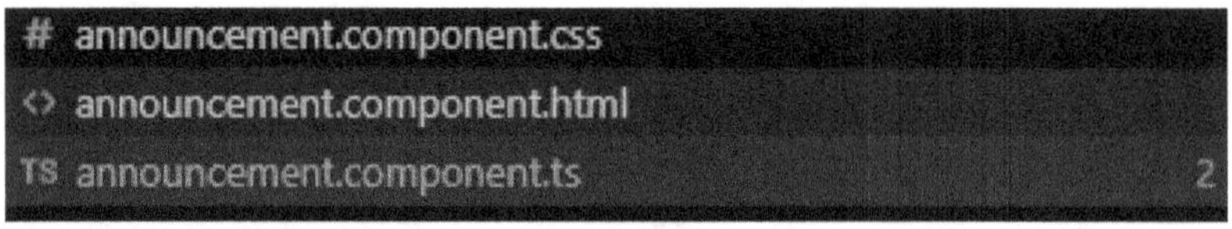

Figure 7-1. Angular file structure

The following is a simple Angular component with screen reader support using the Angular CDK:

```
<div class="container">
    <h1>Status Updates Demo</h1>
```

```html
    <!-- Live region for announcements -->
    <div aria-live="polite" aria-atomic="true" class="sr-only">
      {{ announcement }}
    </div>

    <div class="actions">
      <button (click)="announceSuccess()" type="button">
        Simulate Success
      </button>

      <button (click)="announceError()" type="button">
        Simulate Error
      </button>

      <button (click)="announceLoading()" type="button">
        Simulate Loading
      </button>
    </div>

    <!-- Status display -->
    <div class="status" [attr.aria-live]="statusLevel">
      <p *ngIf="status" [ngClass]="statusClass">
        {{ status }}
      </p>
    </div>
  </div>
```

```css
.container {
    padding: 20px;
    max-width: 600px;
    margin: 0 auto;
  }

  .actions {
    display: flex;
    gap: 10px;
    margin: 20px 0;
  }
```

CHAPTER 7　SPAS AND MODERN FRONT-END FRAMEWORKS AND ACCESSIBILITY

```
button {
  padding: 10px 15px;
  border: 1px solid #ccc;
  background: #f5f5f5;
  border-radius: 4px;
  cursor: pointer;
}

button:hover {
  background: #e9e9e9;
}

button:focus {
  outline: 2px solid #007cba;
  outline-offset: 2px;
}

.status {
  margin-top: 20px;
  padding: 15px;
  border-radius: 4px;
}

.success {
  background: #d4edda;
  color: #155724;
  border: 1px solid #c3e6cb;
}

.error {
  background: #f8d7da;
  color: #721c24;
  border: 1px solid #f5c6cb;
}

.loading {
  background: #d1ecf1;
  color: #0c5460;
  border: 1px solid #bee5eb;
```

```css
  }
  .sr-only {
    position: absolute;
    width: 1px;
    height: 1px;
    padding: 0;
    margin: -1px;
    overflow: hidden;
    clip: rect(0, 0, 0, 0);
    white-space: nowrap;
    border: 0;
  }
```

```typescript
import { Component } from '@angular/core';
import { LiveAnnouncer } from '@angular/cdk/a11y';

@Component({
  selector: 'app-announcement',
  templateUrl: './announcement.component.html',
  styleUrls: ['./announcement.component.css']
})
export class AnnouncementComponent {
  announcement = '';
  status = '';
  statusClass = '';
  statusLevel: 'polite' | 'assertive' = 'polite';

  constructor(private liveAnnouncer: LiveAnnouncer) {}

  announceSuccess() {
    this.status = 'Operation completed successfully!';
    this.statusClass = 'success';
    this.statusLevel = 'polite';

    // Announce to screen readers using CDK
    this.liveAnnouncer.announce('Success: Operation completed
    successfully!');
  }
```

```
  announceError() {
    this.status = 'Error: Something went wrong!';
    this.statusClass = 'error';
    this.statusLevel = 'assertive'; // More urgent

    // Announce error immediately
    this.liveAnnouncer.announce(
      'Error: Something went wrong! Please try again.',
      'assertive'
    );
  }

  announceLoading() {
    this.status = 'Loading... Please wait';
    this.statusClass = 'loading';
    this.statusLevel = 'polite';

    this.liveAnnouncer.announce('Loading content, please wait');

    // Simulate completion after 3 seconds
    setTimeout(() => {
      this.announceSuccess();
    }, 3000);
  }
}
```

This is why this code is good for accessibility:

- Live announcements

    ```
    <div aria-live="polite" aria-atomic="true" class="sr-only">
        {{ announcement }}
    </div>
    ```

    Why this is good:

    aria-live="polite": Screen readers announce changes without interrupting the current speech.

    aria-atomic="true": This announces the entire message, not just the changed part.

.sr-only: It can be visually hidden but available to screen readers.

Dynamic content: Users know when the status changes even if they can't see the screen.

- CDK live announcement service

```
this.liveAnnouncer.announce('Success: Operation completed successfully!');
```

Reliable announcements: It works across different screen readers.

Priority levels: You can use 'polite' versus 'assertive' for different urgency.

No visual disruption: Sighted users aren't bothered by announcements.

Consistent API: The Angular CDK handles the browser differences.

- Dynamic ARIA attributes

```
<div class="status" [attr.aria-live]="statusLevel">

// Error gets immediate attention
this.statusLevel = 'assertive'; // Interrupts current speech

// Success is less urgent
this.statusLevel = 'polite'; // Waits for current speech to finish
```

Errors: Users immediately know when something goes wrong.

Success messages: Success messages don't interrupt users unnecessarily.

Loading states: Users know to wait when something is loading.

- Semantic HTML structure

```
<button (click)="announceSuccess()" type="button">
    Simulate Success
  </button>
```

This is keyboard accessible, screen reader friendly, and has focus management. In addition, the type button prevents users from accidentally submitting the form.

- Visual accessibility

```
.success {
    background: #d4edda;
    color: #155724;
    border: 1px solid #c3e6cb;
}
.error {
    background: #f8d7da;
    color: #721c24;
    border: 1px solid #f5c6cb;
}
```

Why it helps:

Color contrast: Meets WCAG guidelines for readability

Multiple indicators: Color + text + border (not just color alone)

Consistent patterns: Users learn to recognize success/error states

This code meets many WCAG guidelines such as 1.3.1, 1.4.3, 2.1.1, 2.4.3, and 4.1.3. The Angular philosophy is (as stated in their docs) to prefer native elements to re-inventing. For example, use <button>, not <span role="button">. Use as many semantic elements as possible.

Frameworks and Choosing Your Path

After exploring accessibility implementations across Vue, Angular, and React, it becomes clear that each framework offers unique strength and approaches to building web applications. While the fundamentals of accessibility remain the same (semantic HTML, proper ARIA usage, focus management, and screen reader support), each framework shapes how these principles are implemented.

Framework-Specific Strengths

Vue.js excels in making accessibility approachable through its template-driven development model. The framework's reactive template system naturally encourages semantic HTML while making dynamic ARIA attributes straightforward to manage. Vue's single-file components create a clear separation of concerns that simplifies accessibility audits, and the Composition API enables powerful patterns for creating the reusable accessibility logic. For teams that value progressive enhancement and gentle learning curves, Vue provides an excellent foundation where accessibility can be layered in gradually without overwhelming developers.

React offers the most flexibility in accessibility implementation, with its component-based architecture enabling sophisticated accessibility patterns through hooks and custom components. The framework's extensive ecosystem includes mature accessibility-focused libraries like React ARIA and Reach UI, while tools like the React Testing Library naturally encourage accessibility-first testing approaches. React's functional programming paradigm and hooks system provide powerful patterns for managing complex accessibility states, making it particularly well-suited for applications requiring custom accessibility behaviors.

Angular provides the most comprehensive accessibility infrastructure out of the box through the Angular CDK. The framework's enterprise-focused philosophy extends to accessibility, offering battle-tested solutions for complex interaction patterns through services like LiveAnnouncer and FocusMonitor. Angular's dependency injection system and TypeScript integration create robust patterns for scaling accessibility across large applications and teams. For organizations requiring consistent accessibility standards and comprehensive tooling, Angular offers amazing infrastructure support.

Implementation Considerations

Simple to medium applications may benefit from Vue's straightforward approach, while complex applications with custom accessibility requirements might leverage React's flexibility. Enterprise applications often benefit from Angular's systematic approach and extensive infrastructure.

Summary and Conclusion

Whenever framework you choose, keep the following in mind:

- **React, hooks, components, and accessibility:** You learned in this chapter how to use React with accessibility, hooks (useEffect), components, and the ESLINT plugin a11Y that you can use lint your web application.

- **Vue template system:** You learned about Vue and why to use it, as well as the Composition API for creating powerful, reusable accessibility logic.

- **Angular robustness:** You learned about dynamic ARIA attributes and why to use Angular.

You can also use linting and testing tools that each frameworks has in its ecosystem.

The future of web accessibility lies in not choosing the "most accessible" framework but in developing the knowledge and processes that consistently produce accessible applications regardless of the technology stack.

Whether you are building an application with Vue reactive templates, React hooks, or an Angular comprehensive service, the goal remains the same: to create a beautiful digital experience that welcomes and includes all users in our increasingly connected world.

Index

A

Accessibility tree, 27, 28
Accessibility visualization, 50
Accessible audio content
    audio formats, 85
    code example, 85
    for deaf-blind users, 88
    digital experience, 89
    examples, 84
    HTML5 audio elements, 85
    HTML audio player implementation, 85
    inclusive Web, 89
    key features, 87
    primary accessibility barrier, 84
    principles, 89
    screen readers, 87
    transcripts, 84
Accessible color design, 35
Accessible images
    alt text, 53–55
    best practices, 53
    users with visual impairment, 53
Accessible Rich Internet Applications (ARIA) 8, 12, 13, 15
    accessibility feature, 116
    attributes (*see* ARIA attributes)
    definition, 17
    general principle, 17
    live regions, 101
    live polite feature, 130
    roles, 18
    web applications accessibility, 17
Achromatopsia, 46
Alt decision tree, 65, 66
Alternative text (alt text)
    best practices, 55
    contextually relevant, 54, 55
    definition, 53
    necessary context and information, 53
    vague, 54
alt text quality, 58
Angular approach, *see* Angular Component Development (CDK)
Angular Component Development (CDK)
    accessibility
        dynamic ARIA attributes, 137
        live announcement service, 137
        reader support, 136
        semantic HTML structure, 137
        visual accessibility, 138
    @angular/cdk/a11y, 132
    file structure, 132
    screen reader support, 132
Angular robustness, 140
Angular's dependency injection system, 139
ARIA, *see* Accessible Rich Internet Applications (ARIA)
ARIA attributes, 33, 119
    aria-checked and aria-selected, 19
    aria-describedby, 19
    aria-disabled, 19
    aria-expanded, 19

INDEX

ARIA attributes (*cont.*)
    aria-hidden, 19
    aria-label and aria-labelledby, 18
    aria-live, 19
    aria-required, 19
    ARIA roles without behavior, 20
    conflict, 21

B
Bar charts, 48

C
Captions
    CSS, 73
    HTML, 70, 75
    language and controls, 75
    musical cues and atmospheric
        audio, 70
    src, 70
    technical implementation, 70
    VTT file, 70
    WebVTT format, 72
CDK, *see* Angular Component
    Development (CDK)
Color blindness, 36
Colors, 36
Color vision deficiencies (CVD), 46
Colour Contrast Analyser, 49
Component-based architecture, 139
CVD, *see* Color vision deficiencies (CVD)

D
Decorative images, 58–60
Dependency array, 119
Deuteranopia/deuteranomaly, 46

div soup, 108
    accessibility catastrophe, 6–8
    code sample, 5
    <div> elements purposes, 9
    semantic version, 6
    transitioning, 8, 9
Document structure roles, 18
Drop-down navigation menus, 22–25

E
Error handling, 101–104
ESLINT Plugin JSX A11y, 121, 122

F
FocusMonitor, 139
Forms
    connecting with labels, 92–94
    designing, 91
    and error handling, 101–104
    grouping, 94–96
    keyboard navigation, 97–101
    semantic HTML, 92
Framework implementation
    considerations, 139
Framework-specific strengths, 139
Functional images, 60, 61

G
Group images, 63
Grouping forms, 94–96

H
Heat maps, 48
HTML/CSS approach, 65

I, J

Image accessibility
- alt decision tree, 65, 66
- ARIA, 56
- conformance levels and techniques, 57, 58
- image types (*see* Image types)
- POUR, 56
- WCAG, 56

Image maps, 63, 64

Image types
- decorative, 58–60
- functional, 60, 61
- group, 63
- image, 63, 64
- informative, 58
- text, 61, 62

Informative images, 58

K

Keyboard navigation, 97–101

L

Labels and forms, 92–94
Landmark roles, 18
Line chart, 47
LiveAnnouncer services, 139
LiveRegionAnnouncer component, 116
<button> element, 4
<div> element disadvantages, 2–4

M

Multiple ExpandableSection components, 115

N, O

Navigation nav bar with ARIA
- basic structure, 21, 22
- combining HTML and JavaScript, 26–28
- disadvantages, 25, 26
- drop-down navigation menus, 22–25
- model implementation, 28, 30–33

P, Q

Pie/donut charts, 48
POUR concepts, 56
Protanopia/protanomaly, 46

R

React Testing Library, 139
React UI library
- screen readers and basic markup, 108–113
- testing and linting, 120–122
- useEffect and accessibility, 116–120
- useState and accessibility, 114–116

React useState hook, 115
Router.js file, 129

S

Schema.org vocabulary, 12, 13
Screen reader, 100
Screen reader compatibility
- ARIA attributes, 75
- basic accessible media controls, 75
- <button> element, 75
- CSS, 77
- implementation, 83
- JavaScript for dynamic controls, 78

Screen reader compatibility (*cont.*)
    media player controls, 75
    text alternatives, 75
    tools and libraries captions, 84
Screen readers
    advantages, 110
    assistive technologies, 111
    button element, 109
    code disadvantages, 112
    implementation, 110, 111
    <nav> element, 109
    real-world impact, 113
    semantic elements, 108, 109
Semantic HTML, 33, 92
    clear document outline, 2
    foundation, 15
    HTML elements, 1, 2
    importance, 1
    special users, 1
    supporting people with disabilities, 2
SEO with well-structured HTML
    accessibility benefits, 13, 14
    advantages, 10
    alt attribute, 11
    content hierarchy and meaning, 10
    enhanced user experience, 10
    index image content, 11
    link destinations, 11
    Schema.org vocabulary, 12, 13
    semantic elements, 10
    structured navigation, 12
Single-page applications (SPAs)
    complex hierarchy, 107
    dynamic content updates, 107
    <div> elements, 107
    Virtual DOM, 107
SPAs, *see* Single-page applications (SPAs)

T

tabIndex, 97, 98
Tab order, 100
Text images, 61, 62
Tritanopia/tritanomaly, 46
TypeScript integration, 139

U

useEffect accessibility, 116, 118–120
useState accessibility, 114–116

V

Video and audio accessibility
    captions (*see* Captions; Screen readers)
    digital experience, 69
    HTML5, 69
Vue accordion, 124–127
Vue.js
    building accessible applications, 122
    Composition API, 122
    declarative syntax, 122
    reactivity system, 122
    Screen Readers, 123–127
    SPA challenge, 127, 128, 130, 131
    testing and linting, 131
vuejs-accessibility package, 131
Vue reactivity system, 122, 123, 131
Vue template system, 140

W, X, Y, Z

WCAG, *see* Web Content Accessibility Guidelines (WCAG)
WCAG-compatible form, 44
Web accessibility, 140
WebAIM Contrast Checker, 49

Web Content Accessibility Guidelines
(WCAG), 56
   accessibility standards, 35
   charts and samples
      bar charts, 48
      heat maps, 48
      line chart, 47
      pie/donut charts, 48
      testing tools, 49
   colors and forms, 38–43
   comprehensive framework, 36
   contrast analyzers, 49
   contrast ratio for text (WCAG 2.1 SC 1.4.3), 37
   data visualizations and charts, 45–47
   disadvantages, 37, 38
   future trends, 50
   key accessibility improvements, 44, 45
   requirements, 64
   screen reader testers, 49
   use of color (WCAG 2.1 SC 1.4.1), 36
Widget roles, 18

GPSR Compliance

The European Union's (EU) General Product Safety Regulation (GPSR) is a set of rules that requires consumer products to be safe and our obligations to ensure this.

If you have any concerns about our products, you can contact us on

ProductSafety@springernature.com

In case Publisher is established outside the EU, the EU authorized representative is:

Springer Nature Customer Service Center GmbH
Europaplatz 3
69115 Heidelberg, Germany